FINDING YOUR
WRITER'S VOICE

Finding Your Writer's Voice

A GUIDE TO CREATIVE FICTION

THAISA FRANK AND

DOROTHY WALL

St. Martin's Press | *New York*

Grateful acknowledgement is made for permission to reprint selections from the following:

"Those Who Don't" by Sandra Cisneros, from *The House on Mango Street* © 1984 by Sandra Cisneros, published by Vintage Books, a division of Random House, Inc., New York, and Alfred A. Knopf. Reprinted by permission of Susan Bergholz Literary Services, Inc.

"The Ox" by Russell Edson, from *The Childhood of an Equestrian,* © 1973 by Russell Edson, Harper and Row Publishers. Reprinted by permission of Russell Edson.

"I Wake Thinking of Myself as a Man" by Susan Griffin, from *Unremembered Country,* © 1987 by Susan Griffin, published by Copper Canyon Press, Port Townsend, WA. Reprinted by permission of Copper Canyon Press.

"Tisanas #82 and #87 by Ana Hatherly, translated by Jean R. Longland, from *A Cidade das Palavras* © 1988 by Ana Hatherly, Quetzal Ediotres, Lisboa. Reprinted by permission of Ana Hatherly.

"I'm A Depressed Poem" by David Ignatow, from *New and Collected Poems 1970–1985,* © 1986 by David Ignatow, Wesleyan University Press. Reprinted by permission of University Press of New England.

"Incidents" by Danhil Kharms, translated by George Gibian, from *The Man with the Black Coat: Russia's Literature of the Absurd,* Northwestern University Press, Evanston, IL, © 1987 by George Gibian. Reprinted by permission of George Gibian.

"Diary Cows" by Ron Koertge, from *Diary Cows,* © 1981 Ron Koertge, Little Caesar Press. Reprinted by permission of Ron Koertge.

"The Eclipse" by Augusto Monterroso, from *Obras Completas (y otros cuentos),* Ediciones Era, © 1990 by Augusto Monterroso. New translation by William Rodarmor printed by permission of Augusto Monterroso.

"To the Roaring Wind" by Wallace Stevens, from *Collected Poems* by Wallace Stevens, copyright © 1923 and renewed 1951 by Wallace Stevens. Reprinted by permission of Alfred A. Knopf, Inc.

F I N D I N G   Y O U R   W R I T E R ' S   V O I C E .

Production Editor: David Sanford Barr
Copyeditor: Mara Lurie
Designer: Judith A. Stagnitto

Library of Congress Cataloging-in-Publication Data

Frank, Thaisa.
    Finding your writer's voice / Thaisa Frank and Dorothy Wall.
        p.   cm.
    ISBN 0-312-11465-6
        1. English language—Rhetoric.   2. Authorship.   I. Wall, Dorothy, 1926– . II. Title.
    PE1408.F573   1994
    808'.042—dc20   94-13079
                                                  CIP

First Edition: October 1994

10 9 8 7 6 5 4 3 2 1

This book is dedicated
sto the loving memory of my mother,
Gladys L. Frank

And to my father,
Robert W. Frank

they taught me to write the truth
and hear the music in human voices
—THAISA FRANK

For Bill and Lisa
— DOROTHY WALL

CONTENTS

Introduction   xiv

Voice

1. Telling Begins in an Atmosphere of Urgency   3
2. Voice: Your Most Powerful Tool   5
3. The Writer as Singer   8
4. The Importance of Raw Voice   10
5. The Voice as an Instrument   15
6. Inner Listening   20
7. Distilling Voice   24
8. Inviting Accidents   26
9. Listening to the Voice of Childhood   28
10. Public and Private Voices   32
11. The Sound of Colloquial Voice   35
12. The Chorus of Voice   38
13. Who's Speaking?: Voice and Character   41
14. Capturing the Inner Critic   46
15. Learning to Spot the Imposter   49
16. The Writer as Presence   54

17. Becoming a Prose Thief 58

18. Using the Journal Dangerously 61

19. Writing in the Pressure Cooker: Leading Raw
Voice into the Story 65

20. If 68

Story

21. Craft and the Voice of the Story 73

22. Going Deeper into the Story: Voice as
Composer and Instrumentalist 77

23. From Anecdotes to Stories 80

24. Catalysts for the Story: Character-, Plot-, and
Vision-Driven Stories 85

25. Working with Short Forms to Discover Your
Story 90

26. Point of View 97

27. Meeting the First-Person Narrator 103

28. Working with Third Person: Discovering a
Narrative Persona 111

29. Secrets as a Key to Character 117

30. Finding Dialogue through Impersonation 122

31. Voice and Tone 127

32. To Plot or Not to Plot 133

33. Gender Bending, Race Switching, and
Beyond 139

34. Unity: Discovering a Story's Design 145

35. Returning to the Pressure Cooker 152

Revision

36. Revision: Exploding the Myth 159

37. The Art of Reading Your Own Fiction 164

38. Should Dick Have a Beard?: Meeting Your
Editors 169

39. Listening for the Story Editor   173

40. Listening for the Sentence Editor   179

41. The Timing of Revision   184

42. How to Surprise Yourself in the Middle of
Your Story   187

43. Filtering Feedback   191

44. When to Rewrite from Scratch   196

45. Talking to the Stranger: Another Angle on
Revision   200

Keeping Voice Alive

46. Returning to Raw Voice   205

47. Voice over the Long Haul   208

48. Audacity and Ruthlessness: (De)Constructing
a Writer's Life   213

49. The Writer as Character   217

50. Writing during Hard Times   221

51. Some Truths about Truth-Telling   226

52. The Importance of Lying   233

53. Becoming Your Own Sovereign   237

ACKNOWLEDGMENTS

I first want to thank my coauthor, Dorothy Wall, whose excitement and imagination have infused this project at every phase. I began our coauthorship confident that a third writer would actually write this book. This third writer would get up every morning in an excellent mood. She would combine our ideas and voices effortlessly. She would finish the book in a year. What a surprise when this third writer never appeared and I began to learn that each writer's rituals are as singular as voice itself. Fortunately this invisible clone was never needed. Our two voices learned to coexist. We became tolerant of each other's work rhythms. I am extremely grateful to Dorothy for being my companion on this exhilarating journey.

I also want to thank the following writers, colleagues, and friends, for hours of patient listening, advice, and encouragement: Sandy Bails, Brad Bunnin, Jon Carroll, Patricia Dienstfrey, Tom Farber, Lenore Friedman, Steve Kaye, Brenda Kienan, Karen Kevorkian, Elise P. Morgan, Rosalie J. Lamb, Nancy Pietrofesa, Carol U. Lewis, Robin Palanker, Carol Piasante, Steven Poling, Dierdre Snyder, Joan Tollifson, Frances Whitney, and

Martha Graham Wiseman. Members of the Writers Conference on The Whole Earth Electronic Link (the WELL), gave invaluable support. My cohosts in that conference, Joe Flower and Sally Randolph, allowed me to disappear when I needed time. Joyce Jenkins and Richard Silberg kept voice alive through articles in *Poetry Flash*. The Dorset Writers Colony gave me a haven. Sue Smith deserves special thanks for allowing me great freedom as a teacher, and the chance to share techniques I first used in my own fiction. So does Anne Fox for encouraging me, long ago, to write down my ideas about writing.

Anne Dubuisson of the Ellen Levine Literary Agency has guided this manuscript through every stage. I am extremely grateful for her boundless support and enthusiasm. George Witte of St. Martin's Press has provided painstaking, perceptive, hands-on editing. His editorial assistant, Ann McKay Farrell, has answered endless questions and kept track of innumerable details. It's been a pleasure to work with both of them.

My family lived and breathed this book for much longer than they ever expected: My son, Casey Rodarmor, ate many frozen pizzas with aplomb and came up with titles and chapter headings that cheered me up. My father, Robert Worth Frank, offered sound advice based on his own experience as a writer and editor. And my husband, William Rodarmor, has been an admirable example of grace under pressure. In the midst of his own writing, editing, and translation deadlines, he helped with faxes, mailings, gave editorial advice, found misplaced manuscripts, and provided a challenging sounding board. Above all, he listened with all his love and support. I couldn't have written this book without him.

Finally, I want to thank my students, who taught me much more that I ever taught them. They struggled to become the writers they wanted to become and succeeded. They took my suggestions and pushed them to explosive possibilities. They were also wonderful to talk to about the mysterious, often lonely, process of writing fiction. A hundred names come to mind—and a hundred more after that. These writers are the guiding spirit behind this book. I'm grateful to every one of them.

—THAISA FRANK

A C K N O W L E G M E N T S

The path that led to this book is one I could not have found alone. I am deeply grateful to my coauthor, Thaisa Frank, for her extraordinary gifts of imagination, insight, and fresh vision. Her ideas pushed mine, her voice fed my own. Despite endless rewrites, tinkering, wholesale dumping, going back to square one, lost drafts, and incompatible computers, the book emerged—richer for having had two guides. I have been inspired and enriched by our partnership.

The hundreds of students and clients I've had the privilege to work with have also shaped this book in a powerful way. These writers provided an essential laboratory to forge and hone these ideas. My sincere thanks to all of them for their thoughts, questions, puzzlements, humor—and most of all, their voices. Special thanks to Lisbeth Blum, Roy Glassberg, Madeline Moore, Jan Potts, and Sofia Shafquat for allowing me to refer to or quote their writing. My continued appreciation goes to Sue Smith and Liz McDonough at U.C. Berkeley Extension, and to Meera Lester and the staff at Writer's Connection, for giving me the opportunity to teach my workshops and classes.

We've had a wonderful, patient, and wise agent guiding this project, Anne Dubuisson. She managed to balance superb professional skills with personal support in a way few people can, and I appreciate all her efforts. Heartfelt thanks go as well to our editor at St. Martin's, George Witte, who saw the potential in this project when it was still sketchy, and hung in there with us all the way. The book would not be what it is without his astute direction and editorial eye. Thanks to Lee Smith for his thoughtful editorial comments, and to all the people at St. Martin's who have lent their expertise and energy, especially Ann McKay Farrell and Laura Mullen.

My friends and family have offered ideas, encouragement, and a vital listening ear. I'm indebted in particular to Shelley Nelson and Susan Hoffman for their comments on early drafts, and to Susan Page for her warm collegiality and enthusiasm. I remain extremely grateful to Peggy Schaefer and the late Joe Schaefer for their faith in me early on, when it mattered most, and their generous support. My aunt and uncle, the fine singers Nancy and Gordon Ewing, offered invaluable information and insight about the parallels between singing and writing. Thanks to my mother for her interest and creativity, to all my sisters for being there, to my daughter Lisa for being the inspiration she is, and most of all, to my partner Bill Barnes whose editorial acumen, unflagging support, and pasta primavera are appreciated beyond measure.

—DOROTHY WALL

Talking about writing fiction is itself a kind of fiction. A writer writes a story using inspiration, memory, luck, and cunning—and when he or she is done, it's hard to know exactly how the story got written. It may have started with an enigmatic first sentence, or a sure knowledge of the ending. It may have taken twenty drafts or one. The writer never fully unravels the alchemy of the story, because part of the process remains underground. At best, writers talk about visible, remembered signposts along the way.

Nonetheless, writers enjoy telling stories about how they write, and other writers enjoy listening. These stories aren't formulas. They're maps, myths, sources of inspiration, clues for discovering future stories. The seeds of self-destruction are inherent in such stories, for when writers listen to enough of them they replace them with stories of their own, or decide that talking about writing simply isn't useful.

In this book we're telling you a series of stories about how we think stories get written. Our protagonist is voice, that much-touted character in fiction writing. Voice has become a buzz-word in discussions of modern fiction, generating a mystique.

It's what every writer wants to have, what every reader wants to enjoy. But what is voice? How do you develop yours?

Voice is nothing fancy. It's simply the way you, the writer, project yourself artistically. It's the way you draw on yourself as you write—your sense of humor, irony, the way you see people and events, use language, and entertain. And it's the way you use these parts of yourself to tell a story—just the way a singer draws on vocal chords, diaphragm, stomach muscles, and emotion to sing.

It's easy to feel intimidated and wonder: Do I have a voice? The answer is: Of course you do. Every writer has a natural voice, and every natural voice has its own way of telling a story. It has its own rhythm, pace, sense of detail, anecdote, and—if allowed to improvise—this natural voice can discover the story's content and form. Natural voice is like a finger pointing at the moon, but it isn't the moon itself. It takes time, patience, and work to refine this voice into a polished voice that can tell a story. But when your natural voice is allowed to lead the way, the result is a story with fire and spirit.

You won't find your voice by getting up on a podium, taking a deep breath, and trying to sound like a great writer. You find your voice by being yourself, speaking naturally—then learning ways to guide and sharpen this natural voice so it tells a story that enthralls a reader.

Our own experience of voice began, as it does for many writers, with the exuberant, natural voice we had as children. At age nine, Dorothy mesmerized her neighborhood friends as she intoned a monologue from her play "Red Ruby Revenge"— inspired by a red cape she'd found in an old trunk. Thaisa got some fan letters when she published a story called "Turn-About," which was about a seventh-grade boy who wasn't ready to date—modeled after a classmate she was passionately in love with. We accessed voice without knowing it, wrote prolifically, unconcerned with profound questions about what we were doing or the story's form.

But when both of us were in our early teens, sensing that

"real" writing was too close to the raw bone of truth to continue to risk—or that maybe real writing was something other people did, not what we did—we quietly put our work away, for later. And later, much later in our twenties, we began to write again, digging backward to retrieve that first, excited voice of childhood.

We quickly discovered (as most writers do) that the raw exuberant voice which inspires a story or poem doesn't always result in a polished piece of work. And yet if we tried to write by imposing a form from the outside (and both of us did try!), we usually ended up with a story that had characters, descriptions, and dialogue, but no sense of life. Like a fossil, it neither lived nor breathed.

How could we revive that natural storytelling voice? What was the alchemy that transformed bits and dashes of voice—surfacing like uncoded messages—into a coherent whole?

If we hadn't begun to teach, we probably would have continued the dialogue haphazardly—the way many writers do: Working like Braille readers, feeling for language in the dark, we might have found a way to write stories and poems, without ever having to articulate how we gave birth to them. But when we began to teach fiction we soon learned that other writers also struggled with similar tensions. "I *know* the story, but I can't find the voice to *write* it," was one common complaint. "I have great ideas, wonderful first sentences, but I can't put these things together to make a story," was another.

We've each worked with a wide array of writers: published writers, novices, genre writers, lyric surrealists, mainstream writers, hard-core realists, ex-poets looking for exciting fictional forms. In our search for a way to tell all of them something useful, we found that in essence they needed to know the same thing: The natural voice that is yours alone is the best guide to your story's form. When linked with an understanding of craft, your voice will form the story and lead the way.

How does one guide the raw, natural voice so it can tell a

satisfying story? In helping writers answer this question we've always started by being forthcoming about our own struggles with voice and story. In the first section, we suggest ways to release your raw voice, that voice that is natural, spontaneous, and connected to your sense of truth about the world. Once you've tapped into this energized, natural voice, we offer suggestions, in the "Story" section, for how to improvise and refine voice into the form of a story that only you could tell. To discover how your voice shapes a story, we encourage you to experiment with anecdotes and short forms of writing. And we explore the different elements of voice—tone, point-of-view, narration, dialogue, characters—that weave into a story.

It's in revision that writers work most consciously to combine craft with the original impulses of raw voice. In the "Revision" section we stress the importance of recapturing the original excitement of voice as an entrance into revising your story. We also suggest ways to develop your inner editors and use their knowledge to guide your voice. In the final section we encourage you to think about the larger issues of letting your voice evolve, sustaining voice over the long haul, and maintaining a writer's life.

Along the way we suggest inventive exercises, musical excursions, and improvisations. We encourage you to look in strange places for clues and solutions. Throw away the old maps. Engage in a process of trial and error. Listen. Dream. Let yourself explore uncharted territory.

We believe that no matter what kind of writer you are, you will find this book useful. If you're a writer who plans ahead (for instance a mystery writer who preplans plots) you will be surprised, as you use our ideas, to find yourself coming up with moments of improvisation that you hadn't anticipated. If you're an intuitive writer, who begins with an open sense of your story's path, you'll find that your stories have a deeper, interior sense of motion. If you're experimenting with fictional forms, you'll find that focusing on voice frees you from expected structures and ways of writing. And if you're just starting to discover the writer within yourself, our book will help you translate your vision into original stories.

For every writer the leap into voice happens differently— some with an urgent awareness of character, others because a voice in their head starts speaking as they hike through a grove of eucalyptus. Rilke started *Duino Elegies* because he was taking a walk by the sea after receiving an upsetting letter and heard a voice in the wind call: *Who, if I cried, would hear me among the angelic/orders?* Faulkner claimed he wrote *The Sound and the Fury* because he was compelled to follow the image of a little girl climbing up a drain pipe. And John Gregory Dunne says he began his novel *The Red, White and Blue* knowing only the first sentence ("When the hour of the trial began we left the country,") and that the last line of the novel would be either "No," or "Yes." (Four years later, when the novel was finished, the last line turned out to be "No.") We encourage you to wander through this book in your own way—taking detours, stopping where you want to, noticing what excites your voice. And we hope, after you've read our book, you'll write your own stories about voice.

Writing is an alchemical process, and the nature of alchemy is that the final transformation of lead into gold can't be completely explained. All a good sorcerer can do is to push the apprentice in the direction of the cauldrons—and then trust that the apprentice will figure out how to make them bubble. This book is our way of pushing you toward the cauldrons so you can become your own sorcerer. Ultimately the room with the cauldrons exists in a country that only you can enter. With the help of this book you will know more about your natural voice—how to release it, how it unites with craft, and how it evolves into a form. You will be able to write stories telling us about that unique country. No one but you could have written them.

Voice

Telling Begins in an Atmosphere of Urgency

When the circumstances are right you can tell extraordinary stories to complete strangers: If you and I are on a crowded train and have to spend the night in the dining car, we may tell each other the most intimate secrets. And if I'm in a foreign city, talking to someone at a café, I may, in fractured French, relate an amazing incident from my life.

In trains, waiting rooms, and strange hotels, during city black-outs and nighttime vigils, when you lose your keys in the rain and spend the evening at a neighbor's house—incredible stories are exchanged. When strangers meet in an atmosphere that allows for excitement and privacy, they tell each other exactly what matters to them at the time. They speak from the heart, forgetting background details. And listeners, responding from the heart, understand.

Readers are also strangers. They may be meeting you only once, just to read this particular story, and may never meet you again. They don't want to hear what's convoluted, overly private, or extraneous. They want to hear what's important, intimate, and compelling.

Any unusual circumstances can create this sense of urgency.

This was eloquently illustrated to me in 1969, when I was part of the Columbia University revolution. Within hours the university was transformed into a foreign country. Students occupied the buildings, and familiar objects like desks and blackboards lost their previous functions. Classrooms turned into dormitories. Offices turned into headquarters. Pamphlets littered the halls. People shed their roles: Professors were no longer professors, students were no longer students. And everyone walked around having very intimate exchanges, saying whatever was on their minds at the moment.

At one point I walked into a room of an occupied building and met someone I'd known in passing. He was large, overbearing, wore thick glasses that made him look bug-eyed and had a crew cut when it wasn't popular. He was also an expert on rockets, made a satellite that was confiscated by the government when he was twelve, and wrote on higher mathematics. Sitting on the floor, wedged between periodicals, with the tersest of introductions, we began to argue about whether history was determined or free. This wasn't the sort of thing I usually talked about to virtual strangers on first meetings. But within this oddly abstract framework, we confided secrets, passions, and memories. The conversation was swift, urgent, and brief. After five minutes we said good-bye. I never saw him again.

Unusual situations call forth voice. But writers must create these situations themselves. When you write, you have to take a leap and live in an atmosphere of urgency. Urgency that creates instant communication. Urgency that allows for excitement. Urgency that lets you touch your reader. In this book we are going to tell you how your voice can connect you to your own sense of urgency, and how you can use your voice to unearth the details that are important to your story. We'll show you how urgency and voice exist in an intimate relationship, how one calls forth the other. We are going to encourage you to avoid writing from a sense of obligation, and stick to the path of excitement and improvisation. In this atmosphere of compression and intimacy, you will learn that your stories can be trusted.

Voice: Your Most Powerful Tool

What is voice? Does every writer have one? How do you go about finding it?

Your voice is actually a very ordinary thing: It is just who you are, projected artistically. It is often linked to your speaking voice, and your breath, and the rhythms and sense of pace that you draw on when you are too absorbed in what you are saying to listen to yourself from a distance. It is also linked to your body, the language or dialect you spoke in childhood, and whatever naturally interests you. Your voice is how you write when you don't have time to be elegant.

Once, at least once, everyone has had the experience of telling a story well and holding an audience. Maybe you were at a party, and found yourself talking to a group of people. Your voice seemed to hold them, make a direct connection; your words evoked an atmosphere. Or maybe you were in a café having a cup of tea with a friend, and a whole event from childhood unraveled in one piece. Whatever it was that you did then is linked to your voice. The words you chose. The pauses in your breath. Whether you told the story quickly, slowly, angrily, gently. Whether you meandered and went into detail, or got straight to the point. Whether you repeated dialogue, or dwelled on the way rooms looked. Whatever you did then was it—this thing called voice.

When you are able to harness it, voice is a powerful tool. It allows you to take readers wherever you want them to go—often to places that are perilous. It conveys your sense of story with authority. It allows you to get your readers to believe anything. Unlike style, voice can never be imitated. It is like a fingerprint, unique and singular.

Nobody but you has your voice. Yet voice isn't unchanging, nor is it a static, precious commodity. It's always shifting in response to an immediate moment, an intention, an audience. Just as you aren't a static, singular entity, neither is your voice.

Because it belongs to you, your own voice is hard to identify. When it comes to knowing who you are, you are often the last to find out. Most writers struggle to unearth voice—not only because one's own voice is simply too familiar, but also because to speak from your voice means confronting your world, your dreams, and your entire life raw and unsoftened by explanations. This is the world of direct, unfiltered experience, sensate impressions, and emotions. To find this world you must be willing to seize the unconventional, the unadorned.

Here's an example: For years, I was haunted by a fight my parents had when I was a child, in which my father—quite eloquently—threw a garbage bag of carrot peels against the wall and turned our kitchen into an art gallery. Again and again, I saw the white wall, the bag of garbage, my father's arms, the criss-cross maze of carrot peels. These images were inaudible, like scenes from a silent movie, and I had no desire to search for any language that could tell their story. This self-censorship came not so much from a desire to protect my family, but from ideas about what kind of writer I wanted to be. (Too psychological, I thought, when considering the images as material for a story. Possibly self-pitying and pathetic.) Then one day, I heard a voice saying: *One day my parents had a fight. My mother threw a clock, and my father threw garbage.* My choices after that were two: to take the leap and write the remaining sentences, or to resist. I chose to leap and wrote a story in which I learned something I hadn't known: that this particular fight was a phenomenal theatrical experience, and that I, as a spectator, had enjoyed it.

Another story started by accident—but again a phrase began it. For some time, I heard in my mind the phrase *the bloodwell*. The phrase felt unpleasantly surreal, and I shoved it aside. However, at some point, because the phrase (and the voice that spoke the phrase) haunted me, I decided to take the image literally. As though I were moving into a fluid abstract sculpture, I suddenly could see a well of blood, with shifting translucent shapes. I could feel it surrounded by human activity.

By following the voice and surrendering to it, I discovered significant images—images that contained the core emotional charge of the story I wanted to tell and that unpacked like a series of Russian nesting dolls, allowing me to improvise with relative ease.

A search for voice must always involve a willingness to experience what you already know in a new light. It doesn't matter whether the objects in your world are unaesthetic, beautiful, ordinary, or extraordinary. The key is to become aware of them.

Take some time to notice patterns, sounds, and objects in your everyday life. Look at the floor of your closet. Notice the paper bag flapping on the parking meter near your office. Listen to the phrases that occur to you before you drift off to sleep. Touch the rough concrete post by a neighbor's meadow. You'll find an abundance of images and ideas in things you've taken for granted. This receptive approach to the familiar is the beginning of the discovery of voice.

The Writer as Singer

In every writer there lurks a singer. It's that voice you had before you ever spoke. One so natural, it was spectacular—full of innate operatic ability. I remember my daughter at nine months gripping the rails of her crib and belting out a wail that shook the neighborhood. Her voice had an authority you couldn't ignore. Fists red, eyes clenched, she cried with an all-consuming bodily passion, worthy of a diva.

Like an opera singer, a baby's whole body works in coordination to produce those piercing cries. The stomach and chest muscles are tight and hard, creating pressure in these body cavities that in turn creates the perfect acoustical atmosphere to amplify sound. The baby's throat is open, offering an unimpeded channel for this pressurized air. The tongue lies flat and vibrates as the air is forced over it, further amplifying and projecting the sound. When the body is such a perfect instrument, sound is pure feeling. Emotion pours from the diaphragm, lungs, fingers, toes.

It's ironic that adult singers have to do breathing exercises for years to learn how to use their bodies the way babies do naturally. Writers, too, have to reach back to that lusty first voice completely in harmony with body, heart, and breath. The natural connection between emotion and sound produces rhythm, force—and gets a response.

Hold this page in front of you like sheet music, stand up straight, and sing the following sentence as if you were an operatic star, with full, emotion-drenched voice:

Maria Velázquez was born on the first of December.

Throw your voice at the wall across the room. Sing it slowly, plaintively. Then huffily, with great impatience. Then enthusiastically, as if you'd just spotted a friend in a crowd. Feel how you use your whole body to produce sound: how you straighten your spine, flex your stomach muscles, widen your rib cage, open your throat. Feel how emotion moves through your body.

If you feel tense, stand and shake your arms and legs. Loosen your neck, tongue, lips. Jump up and down. Relax those muscles in your shoulders. Breath from your diaphragm. Yawn. Cry. Laugh.

Open the Bible at random, put your finger on a verse and read aloud, listening to the prose as if it were music. Now sing a passage. What kind of singer are you? A blues singer, with an empty heart? A rapper, sizzling with energy? An opera singer at the head of an extravagant processional? Let your voice expand, resonate.

When your singing voice is loose, your writing voice will be, too. Read a passage of your own writing. What kind of music is it? Sing it like German lieder, or rock music, or a classical ballad.

Now do the same thing with four very different writers, say Charles Dickens, Anaïs Nin, Raymond Carver, and Gabriel García Márquez. Whose language would you use to hurl at someone in a fight? Whose would you use to tell a secret? To paint a room?

The Importance of Raw Voice

Voice, of course, is a complete and complex orchestra; but for the purpose of talking about the process of creating fiction, it's helpful to talk about two aspects of voice—raw voice and a voice that can tell a whole story. The voice that can tell a whole story is more polished than raw voice, those phrases that just float up to you: *A train to the end of the world. My father throwing garbage. My great-aunt shaking hands while sitting on the toilet. Joanie done got her car stolen.* They're the phrases that you don't consciously solicit or control.

The voice of the story utilizes raw voice. It is what happens to raw voice when it is working with narrative, shape, and form. The voice of the story can work in different forms: spin yarns, evoke images, speak in tongues, write sometimes lyrically, sometimes matter-of-factly. It can write a story or a poem, a screenplay or a novel. It can tell the stories of infinite characters.

R A W V O I C E

Raw voice is available to anyone who is human. It uses natural language and often is connected with a sense of urgency and honesty about what is being said. It occurs when people speak as well as when they write, and no one has a corner on it. The following statement by the Italian immigrant and anarchist Bartolomeo Vanzetti, made after he and Nicola Sacco were sentenced to death for allegedly murdering two men, is an eloquent expression of raw voice:

> *If it had not been for these things, I might have live out my life talking at street corners to scorning men. I might have die, unmarked, unknown, a failure. Now we are not a failure. This is our career and our triumph. Never in our full life could we hope to do such work for tolerance, for joostice, for man's onderstanding of man as now we do by accident. Our words—our lives—our pains—nothing! The taking of our lives—lives of a good shoe-maker and a poor fish-peddler—all! That last moment belongs to us—that agony is our triumph.*
> —APRIL 9, 1927

You may have intellectual judgments about Vanzetti's guilt or innocence, but your heart cannot argue with the deep sense of connection he is making. Vanzetti can't spell everything correctly. He hasn't mastered the English language. But his inner spirit is there and spirit can't be argued with.

It's important to remember that raw language often contains the seeds of vision—the unique way that each writer sees the world—and that vision inspires language. In this way voice and vision are inseparable: By paying attention to one, you can begin to access the other. Raw voice is a key to vision, because it contains material that is close to what people really think and feel about their experiences. For this reason raw voice often manifests in those very phrases (as well as images and kinesthetic sensations) which seem boring, childlike, or naive. In some sense the ability to capture raw voice comes from a willingness to listen to the unremarkable. It also means listening to something that is close to you.

THE VOICE OF THE STORY

The voice of the story has its seeds in raw voice, but takes the voice one step further—into a realm where it is possible to improvise and, in the process of improvisation, produce a piece that has momentum and unity. This voice is what every writer wants and needs. You cannot write well without it. Here is an example of the voice of the story—a voice that uses raw material, but weaves it into a vision, a unity, a whole.

THE OX

There was once a woman whose father over the years had become an ox.

She would hear him alone at night lowing in his room.

It was only one day when she looked up into his face that she suddenly noticed the ox.

She cried, you're an ox!

And he began to moo with his great pink tongue hanging out of his mouth.

He would stand over his newspaper, turning the pages with his tongue, while he evacuated on the rug.

When this was brought to his attention he would low with sorrow, and slowly climb the stairs to his room, and there spend the night in mournful lowing.

—RUSSELL EDSON

This is the refined writer's voice at work—the voice that can tell a whole story. It moves from a beginning to an end, carefully developing a range of significant images. Notice how deftly Edson seizes authority and gets you to believe this impossible situation. The father is lowing. The father is turning the pages of the newspaper with his tongue.

The voice of the story doesn't try to analyze or explain. Edson's logical mind may help him shape his material, but it doesn't take over or control the story. Instead, the raw voice propels the story. He gets us to see the poignant father-ox, turning the newspaper with his tongue, defecating in the living room. We don't know if he was writing about his father, his wife's father, or himself as a father. We don't know whether he originally dreamt the story—nor do we care. He lets the images take him wherever they need to go.

G E T T I N G T O K N O W
Y O U R I N S T R U M E N T

Beginning writers often forget the importance of letting their raw voice lead the story. They start with the voice of the story, often some other writer's story, and hope it will yield powerful, original material. But this is like trying to compose before you know whether you are composing for a piano or an oboe, perhaps before you even know how a piano or an oboe works. You have to learn your basic instrument first.

Getting to know your raw voice is a perilous process—one that all writers embark on when they start to learn their craft. How do you play such an instrument? Do you sing its scales? Do you tell its stories? Go back to its origins? Revive its history? Or do you simply learn a new way of listening? Chances are that most writers do a combination of these things, as well as finding unique methods (often impossible to articulate) for identifying raw voice when it's there.

In the second section of this book we will grapple with the

exciting process of working with raw voice and the more polished voice of the story simultaneously. We'll help you develop a personal alchemy, in which you channel the material of raw voice into a voice that can weave a narrative whole. But first we're going to explore raw voice in depth. Like the stories in *A Thousand and One Nights,* raw voice has many aspects and keeps unfolding in new guises. We hope you will learn to play with it, revel in it, and trust it.

The Voice as an Instrument

What syllable are you seeking,
Vocallissimus,
In the distances of sleep?
Speak it!

— WALLACE STEVENS

First and foremost voice deals with sound, quite apart from meaning. When you write, you hear the sounds of the words subliminally. When you speak, you feel vibrations in your body. These sounds are connected to a web of meaning, and you can never disengage from that web completely. With a little practice, however, you can return to the experience of your voice as an elemental instrument.

In a letter to Eugène Lefébre, (May 17, 1867), Mallarmé said:

> *I think the healthy thing for man—for reflective nature—*
> *is to think with the whole body; then you get a full har-*
> *monious thought, like violin strings, vibrating in unison*
> *with the hollow wooden box. But I think that when*
> *thoughts come from the brain alone (the brain I abused so*
> *much last summer and part of last winter), they are like*
> *tunes played on the squeaky part of the first string. . . .*
> *On Easter day I got a terrible headache from thinking only*
> *with my brain, after I had gotten it going with coffee;*

> *because it can't get going by itself, and my nerves were*
> *probably too tired to respond to any outside impression; I*
> *tried to stop thinking that way, and with a tremendous*
> *effort I braced the nerves in my chest so as to produce a*
> *vibration—still holding on to the thought I was then*
> *working on. . . . Ever since then, whenever the crucial*
> *hour of synthesis approaches, I say to myself: "I am going*
> *to work with my heart"; and then I feel my heart . . . and*
> *the rest of my body is forgotten, except for the hand that*
> *is writing, and the living heart, and my poem is begun—*
> *begins itself."*

Mallarmé understood that the whole body participates in the creation of voice. He also sensed that where voice resides (or is placed) in the body affects the quality of writing. Some writers readily grasp the connection between voice and the body. But if you tend to think of writing as a purely mental act, Mallarmé's model may help you.

In the seventies, I taught journal workshops to students who practiced yoga, chanted mantras, and never let a class go by without doing neck exercises. When I told them "Voice is sound," they looked at me strangely. They didn't need an explanation for something they instinctively understood.

The same year, however, I worked with a group of college professors who were feeling blocked with their academic writing. They were fascinated to discover the role the body plays in language. Somewhat tentatively (and quoting Mallarmé for ballast), I explained to them that in yoga each part of the body is assigned a special sound, and sometimes people strengthen their awareness of the body by chanting these sounds. Far from being skeptical, they wanted to know the syllables and asked that we spend time in class chanting. I didn't want to appear to be a crackpot, so I led them hesitantly, chanting softly. Almost immediately, everyone went into a trance. In particular I have a vivid memory of an elderly dean, sitting cross-legged on the floor, rocking back and forth, with his eyes closed. Later he reported hearing a lyric passage—his first experience with raw, natural voice. This passage became the first paragraph of a story. Eventually his academic writing began to come more easily. "Why?" I asked. "I don't know," he answered. "Maybe my more personal writing found another outlet. Maybe I just relaxed about it."

If you're curious, you can begin to experiment with your own voice as an instrument: Like Mallarmé, you can make your voice resonate from different parts of your body and discover the different emotions and sounds that arise. Take a leap of faith and believe that each part of your body can speak. Imagine that your entire body is a vehicle for speech and sound—a luminous and versatile transmitter. Let your stomach write a paragraph. Then your heart. Now let your forehead speak. Does your writing change as your body focus shifts? Are the rhythms different? The emotions? The sounds?

In the process you may become aware of the role breath plays in human speech. Breath creates natural pauses between thoughts and the sense of true silence between paragraphs. Furthermore, breathing deeply can help you connect to emotions, and emotions help you connect to language. (A number of writers, myself included, have discovered that shallow breathing accompanies periods of feeling stymied or blocked.) Write a paragraph holding your breath and see how hard that is.

I M I T A T I N G   T H E   F L O W
O F   S P E E C H

Writing structured, resonant nonsense can help you imitate the flow and spirit of human speech. This is another way to discover voice as an instrument, and language as a form of play, freed from the burden of meeting. The rules are simple: 1) the sentences must be grammatical, and 2) the words mustn't link together in any *consciously* associative way. (The mind automatically makes sense of grammatical language. Don't worry if the exercise "makes sense" or the phrases carry metaphoric weight when you read them over.)

This is a halfway point between giving voice complete freedom and working within some kind of structure. Like Lucky, who made an outrageously nonsensical speech in *Waiting for Godot*, you can mimic language, savor the pure sound of words out of context, revel in their absurdity, feel bound and even challenged by the limits of grammar. You're only working with individual sentences at this point, but this exercise may give you a glimpse into more sophisticated uses of improvisation you will need later, when you work on a complete story.

Here's an example:

> *Although spoons create kymographic leaves, the undulating verve of the bracken riveted rice, and when the callous failed, luminous clacks vied the loom with a sandwich; but the miracle mill-raced on, and a liver starch gave in to gibbous grommets—so it wasn't before the onerous futhark of climbs unfurled. And once, when the bombastic fungi lubricated the switch-yard, imperilment was delayed. Ladder! Units! The potash massacre is electrolyzed!*

Everybody finds their own way of writing nonsense. Some people begin by looking around their room and choosing various objects. Others look up words in the dictionary. Others make up nonsense syllables. Some people scan memory, finding words from different phases in their life. Others go into a kind of dream state. Whatever you do may give you insight into your creative process.

Various benefits can emerge from this exercise: Many people report that they actually experience their voice as a musical instrument, independent from meaning. They suddenly discover an urge to work with cadence, rhythm, alliteration. Others say they go on a kind of archaeological dig, excavating voices inside of them, uncovering layers of their own language systems. (I wrote for a while in the rhythms of Old English. Others find themselves writing in dialects or the voices of grandparents.) Some find phrases that suggest stories or stumble on the voice of characters. Also, the inner critic—that insufferable backseat driver—often becomes distracted by assisting in nonsense and later, when you sit down to write a first draft of a story, will stop interrupting with sensible questions. Unfettered by meaning, voice begins to take you where it wants to go. You begin to make new links between words, use sentences you never dreamed of.

Inner Listening

A beginning African musician concentrates all his energy on listening to his own rhythm, and only his own rhythm. Eventually, as he becomes more proficient, the student reaches a point where the drum is said to beat itself. Only then is he allowed to listen to the rest of the music. And only then is he considered a drummer.

—MICKEY HART, *DRUMMING AT THE EDGE OF MAGIC*

There's really no mystery to learning to listen for your inner voice. It's simply a matter of paying attention, of throwing off ideas about what your voice should say and letting it speak for itself. It's a matter of moving inside yourself, plunging into the whirl and depth of your innermost being—into the wilderness, the part you don't know. There's a great deal of wisdom in there. Listen. Quiet the noise around you. Don't reach for voice. Let it reach for you.

This kind of listening is an act of faith: faith that your voice is there, that it will emerge, and that what it says matters. If you're lucky, this faith is present from the beginning of your life as a writer. Your inbred knowledge of an inner voice may be the initial spur to write. You wake up with a sentence running through your head, and know it's the beginning of a story. Hearing an inner voice is as natural to you as breathing.

Often, though, you have to conjure this faith. And ironically, the best way to do this is by starting to write. Singers talk about the moment of trepidation before they utter their first note. Standing before the audience, a deep hush descends. They fear their voice will desert them and nothing will come out. Then the first phrase acts like an engine. Breath, instinct, and emotion take over, and the other notes follow with a momentum of their own.

You can stew and fret about your inner voice—Do I have one? Does it have something to say?—but once you make the leap and start writing, you abandon yourself to the moment, unconcerned with outcomes. You become seized by a delicious gravity that pulls you into a realm of surprises and strange turns: unimagined words and phrases roll forward.

One of the best ways to send yourself past the fear of the cliff edge and into that exhilarating freefall is through "freewriting": writing that you do completely as a kinesthetic act, with no thought, no care for what emerges. Simply put pen to paper and write nonstop for five minutes at first, then ten, and eventually twenty minutes or longer. Write whatever leaps into mind, whether silly, mundane, repetitive, nonsensical. If you hit a blank, write, "I can't think of anything to write, I can't think of anything to write, I can't think of . . ." until other words, by the sheer energy of your pen's movement, are pulled forth. If you trust the act itself, you'll find you can reach a fluid inner energy, a place where language erupts spontaneously.

Take a deep breath. Listen for a rhythm, a feeling, an inner hum. Now begin writing. Delight in the sounds and sentences that drift up . . . *the hour and the second hand, the long slow lung, the fast sweep, fast beep, fast heart, dark rum, sassafras, blue bark, float a drum, hum, hum. . . .*

If you start by listening for voice as pure sound, not worrying about what it's saying, you'll discover a special kind of receptivity that lets voice arise more easily. Revel in the gibberish and chatter: you're warming up, loosening your inner instrument. When you feel the exuberance of voice, you'll find you move naturally from a voice that is pure sound to a voice that carries content. You'll stumble onto characters, images, scenes.

Here's a variation: Start your freewriting with a word or phrase that is particularly evocative for you: *drizzle, key, lemon,*

*animal skins, disguised as the overstuffed chair, never blinked his
eyes when he was dreaming.*

RITUALS FOR CULTIVATING VOICE

You can learn to pay attention to those moments when voice is
spontaneously activated, to those sentences or phrases that
spring to mind as you're pinching melons in the grocery store
or cleaning out the basement. Be on the alert. These are wonderful offerings.

You can also learn to cultivate voice, to deliberately encourage its presence, to set its fuse. As the story goes, playwright
Friedrich von Schiller did his best writing when he could smell
the rotting apples he kept in his desk drawer. I sometimes have
my students sprawl on the floor with a long sheet of butcher
paper and crayons before they begin writing. In a short time
they're engrossed in color and shape, elbowing each other and
fighting territorial wars. The sweeping, fluid movement of that
waxed crayon on the page makes them forget they're supposed
to be writers. Later, when they begin to play with words, they're
looser, more relaxed.

Anything that helps you get out of your head and be playful
will help you access voice. Forget about writing the great American novel. Be outrageous. Experiment. The more freedom you
feel, the more freedom your voice will feel. Try these rituals to
invoke your voice. Invent your own.

1. Write in the dark or with your eyes closed.
2. Dress all in one color and write.
3. Use meditation or relaxation techniques to clear your
head of interference, of white noise.
4. Steam some rose petals or ginger root near your writing
desk; write outdoors among pine needles or wild herbs; find
other ways to activate odors that move you.

5. Play. Don't think of writing a scene or a story. Write fragments, pieces of dialogue, scattered phrases. Don't worry about how they'll fit together.

6. Cut up the lines or paragraphs you've written. Stir them up, rearrange them.

7. Surround yourself with favorite or evocative objects as you write.

8. Cross-dress (as a man if you're a woman, as a woman if you're a man) and write.

9. Hum an inner rhythm as you write. Change that rhythm and see how your writing changes.

10. Write when you're angry. Write when you're tired. Write when you're bored (jealous, sad, excited, etc.).

11. Draw pictures before you begin writing, with crayons or watercolors. Lose yourself in the colors and shapes.

12. Write with your left hand if you're right-handed, with your right hand if you're left-handed.

An added benefit from these experiments: You may find that as you invoke your voice in different ways, you're encouraging it to appear in various guises and moods. Your voice's tone and rhythm may change when you write dressed all in red, or when you write in the dark! These exercises can help stretch your voice's range, perhaps encourage characters to speak.

Distilling Voice

This recipe for freewriting helps you reduce your writing to essentials. It also helps you develop your inner ear, your instinctive response to those places in your writing that are charged. Like the musician who can hear where the music is resonant, you begin to sense where your writing is on. You can hear it. As you do this, you're zeroing in on the parts of your writing that are alive, vital—those places where you want to push further. You begin to recognize language that is deeply connected to the body and insists upon being heard and remembered.

1. Write without stopping for ten minutes each day for a week. Let this be a real freefall. Write at top speed, without thinking, without judging, without editing. What you write each day can be a discrete piece, or you can continue with the same piece.

2. Now put these exercises away and take a week off. Don't look at what you wrote during this time. Let it rest. After a week, go back and read aloud what you wrote in those ten-minute periods. As you read, mark the words, phrases, or passages that leap out at you, that grab your attention.

3. Begin the ten-minute daily writing exercises again, *beginning each time with one of your marked phrases or words.* Using your most exciting writing as your point of departure helps you avoid introductions and leap right into what's vital.

Do this each day for another week. Then put what you've written away.

4. After another week has passed, go back to the second batch of writing and again read aloud, marking those passages that are charged, provocative, unusual. Now delete everything you haven't marked. Read the remaining passage aloud. You should be left with what really sings. If the writing still feels weak or diluted, repeat the process.

You may end up with a prose poem, a surprising non sequitur with its own sense of wholeness, a surreal story, humorous nonsense. Consider this one of your best pieces of writing. Pin it above your desk. Let it inspire you.

Inviting Accidents

I don't draw. I begin by making all sorts of blots. I wait for what I call "the accident": the blot with which the painting can begin. . . . They're "things that happen to me," that happen through me, through my nervous system . . .

— FRANCIS BACON, IN AN INTERVIEW
WITH MARGUERITE DURAS

Improvisational freewriting—even when focused, like the exercise in distilling voice, or when structured, like the exercise in grammatical nonsense—can produce a lot of off-the-wall nonsense, clichés, directionless rambling. But it may allow you to stumble on something else as well: an "interesting accident"— a spontaneous phrase or sentence that excites you, makes you feel you're onto something. Suddenly the language holds a charge. You feel a spark of excitement through your body. Your voice has transmitted its own energy back to you.

These words are a product of the nervous system, rather than the mind, and their unpredictability is their magic. They're electric, unrehearsed, and freewrites are only the beginning of their discovery. Indeed, once you train your ear to recognize them, you'll discover interesting accidents everywhere—in the last paragraph of a muddled first draft, in the voice of a character saying, "I always bake bread with my coat on," in a story you remember from childhood. One might say that these "ink blots" of voice (what random shapes were to the artist Francis Bacon) are the key to finding significant events in your fiction—i.e. those events that suggest other events, introduce characters, and propel you into narrative. Almost invariably, when this charged material is culled and used with focus, it catalyzes a story, or provides some elemental building blocks—or does both.

Here's an example of what we mean. For a long time I was captivated by the words *dream envy*—so captivated, I wrote them down and pinned them above my desk. The phrase remained above my desk for nearly two years—opaque, resonant, mysterious—until one day, when an editor had asked me to write a story about childbirth and I was feeling stumped, I noticed the phrase again. As I looked at it, I imagined a serenely happy man and an angry, pregnant woman lying in bed. He was telling her a dream and she was seething with envy.

Without knowing it, I'd made a leap from a two-word phrase into the first scene of a story. I'd also created two characters— one who provoked the envy of dreams and another who was susceptible. The phrase, *dream envy,* was only a seed: It took a long time for the story to unravel. But if I hadn't allowed myself to be fascinated by it, that phrase never would have been a catalyst for a story.

Freewrites help you develop a vital relationship to your voice: They trick you into losing control, help you shake loose from external manipulations. They give you a chance to stumble on those interesting accidents which later can become significant events in your fiction, and focal points for improvisation. Write a lot of them, invent variations of your own, and don't worry if a few of them yield nothing. The beauty of freewrites is that they have a throw-away quality, and there's no right or wrong way to do them.

Listening to the Voice
of Childhood

When my aunt came back from England after the war, we all went to New York to visit her. She had been in the WACs—something that made me think she'd been allowed to wack soldiers—and her olive-drab suitcases cluttered my grandmother's bedroom. One day we sat on one of the trunks, tucked in a corner by a window. It was raining, a light spring rain. The moment felt very special to me, almost secret. I told my aunt I would tell her a story, and she said that she'd love to hear one. We sat on the trunk in silence, and I looked around—at the white hobnail bedspread on the rosewood bed, a dresser with a rosewood mirror, my aunt's trunks and olive-drab clothes: I couldn't think of a thing to say. My aunt waited. I happened to notice the sweater I was wearing—a dark green cardigan with brass buttons. I took a breath: "Once upon a time there was a family of mice who wore green sweaters and ate hot cereal. They lived in a mouse hole and were very happy."

Right then, I learned one of the important tenets of fiction: Say what's on your mind and improvise with authority. I was greatly assisted by my aunt—one of the luminous, patient listeners of my childhood. I was also helped by my own voice, which followed the line of narrative unselfconsciously, with my very breath. When I couldn't think of anything to say, the words trailed off. When ideas came quickly, the words tumbled over each other. Lulls expressed transition, rushes expressed excitement. The images I chose were sensory, concrete. The mice did whatever occurred to me.

All children are natural storytellers and natural improvisors. Their stories may seem fragmented, or clichéd; but they're almost always compelling because they're told with spontaneity and freedom. Children naturally choose images that are connected to their emotions—and such images are richly alive, full of interesting accidents. Here is a story once told to me by a three-year-old girl:

> *Once upon a time there was a pig who climbed up the ceiling on a little string and flied around and flied around and flied around. He flied all around the room and was a bery nice pig.* [Pause. Impasse. No ideas at all. At this point she began to stare at a nearby lamp. Suddenly she continued.] *Anyway, this pig wanted to get married so he could have a lamp to read. But the lamp said "I don't want to live with no pig." Poor pig. He couldn't see to read. This is a bery sad story.*

As she talked her voice naturally conveyed the shape and movement of the story—the pig's desire for the lamp, his sadness about the lamp's saying "no." She didn't overexplain and expressed her images with surety. Each word was propelled by her breath; the story came from her body in gasps, starts, stops. I could see the courtship of the lamp and the pig—brief but poignant.

Children haven't learned to censor, nor have they cut themselves off from breath. Also—maybe most important—they haven't cut themselves off from their passions. For this reason their vision of life goes right to the core and their anecdotes often explode into a natural sense of narrative, seemingly effortless improvisation. They talk about what's urgent to them at the moment.

When you were a child and didn't get to go to the circus, you knew it mattered. You remembered the rain on the cottonwood tree, the raspberry tarts your mother made as a way of making up for it, the fact that your father was reading and refused to taste them. This wasn't an idea of an event modeled after John Le Carré or Margaret Atwood or Henry James. Incidents that were important to you arose from the flux of your life, and so did your stories. You zeroed in on what mattered—and these potent events and images propelled your story forward.

Try these exercises:

1. Tell a brief story, using images from the room you're in, the sounds you hear, your view out of the window. Don't think about where the story is going or its subject matter. Just tell the story, letting your eyes, ears, and body sensations guide you. Allow yourself to improvise, or—as we said when we were children—"make things up." Now write a couple of stories, using the same technique. Don't worry if the stories seem primitive: their content and sense of momentum may surprise you.

2. The places where we talked as children—especially to other kids—are often a very important influence on childhood speech. When I was in grade school, my best friend and I always told dirty jokes on the playground or in someone's bedroom. But we saved important, heartfelt confidences for under the porch, often while we were shelling peas for dinner. See if you can travel back to the corners, the streets, the gardens, the vacant lots, the attics—those places where you daydreamed alone and spoke to other children. When you go back there, try to set aside your adult voice and speak as you did at the age you were. Talk (or write) about anything you want to. If you can't remember a setting, create one in your imagination.

3. Experiment with breath: Try telling a story and imagine

that someone is interrupting you. Now tell the same story in one breath.

4. Experiment with using your senses, particularly senses you tend to ignore: Go into a supermarket with no intention of shopping, and concentrate on listening. Go to a musical event and watch the people. Open the door to your house and sense your body as it moves through hallways, rooms, dark closets, rummages through drawers.

These excursions can unearth memories that are pleasant or painful. They can even yield stories. But the purpose of these archaeological digs isn't therapy or polished fiction, and there's no need to guide them toward epiphany or revelation. When we speak about returning to the voice of childhood we don't mean a return to childhood memories. We're just speaking about returning to the qualities of childhood voice—fluid, uninhibited access to language, connection to breath, natural cadence, and the automatic ability to discern what is important. We're also speaking about a return to the ear of childhood, an ear which heard music in the human voice, and truth conveyed by voices around you. In this sense, these exercises are doors to a forgotten voice, a voice that is intimately connected to your body and your heart, a voice that first told you about the world.

Public and Private Voices

When my son was two-and-a-half and first learning to talk, I never got tired of listening to him. I might be cooking in the kitchen, or sitting at my desk, when suddenly I'd hear a monologue that sounded like something from James Joyce's *Ulysses: Cat bells. Cat bells. Today's tomorrow. I don't like all da peoples. Cat bells. Cat bells. Name's Case. . . .* While he delivered these soliloquies he often moved around the house— patting a stuffed animal, looking out the window, eating a spoonful of yogurt. He also had wonderful, unexpected names for objects—"thumb-toe" for big toe, and "drumbone" for chicken leg.

Like all children, my son didn't make a strong distinction between what he said alone and what he said in the presence of other people. His colloquial language was fused with his inner world and he made almost no separation between his public and private life. This is the case for all of us when we're young, and it's one reason that children have such rich, surprising language. But as we grow up and become more public, we learn to censor. In most cases, the public voice takes over and the private voice goes underground, receding into dreams, fantasies, unnoticed internal monologues—what we sometimes call the "life of the imagination." The result is that when many writers start to draw material from their inner world, their language is stilted, unnatural, not in harmony with the breath—and much too lofty. It's almost as though we're afraid to return to a time when we spoke our most private thoughts out loud, and reach too far in the other direction, trying to sound literary and grown-up. Here are a few exercises that may be helpful:

1. When you know you're going to be alone, walk around your house, and talk or sing about anything you want to. Do this a few times on different days. Don't try to impose a story or a narrative. Experiment with weaving back and forth between your inner world and what you notice in the house.

2. Close your eyes and daydream out loud.

3. Borrow a stuffed animal. Tell it a story. Do the same thing with a pet.

4. Remember or imagine a time when you were small enough to talk out loud—knowing that another person was in earshot, yet not concerned with what they thought or whether they listened. Say whatever occurs to you.

5. Choose at least one of the above exercises and transcribe what you say. Put it in a drawer. Read it a month from now. (Hint: All writers should be aware of the maturity value of the desk drawer. It's like a ripening bin, or a wine cellar. If you store your work for a while and look at it later, you'll often discover new possibilities.)

As you experiment with these monologues, you may find that the boundaries between public speech and private speech begin to feel more fluid. Elements of your imagination and dream life—previously thought too absurd for public view—may creep into your stories. This exercise is particularly helpful for writers who draw heavily on lyric elements and surreal events. But even writers who tend to rely on material from what we call "real life" may broaden their territory.

The Sound of Colloquial Voice

A famous writer was told, after giving a lecture: "You talk just the way you write." Her answer was: "It took me years."

The language that's most accessible to everyone is the language that you speak every day—what you say to your daughter when you want her to turn off the TV, to a driver who's cut you off at an intersection, to a friend with a toothache. Like the language of childhood, colloquial language is close to breath and rhythms of the body. You hear it and speak it without knowing much about it. This language isn't the polite, borrowed voice of formal conversation or public milieus. It's the relaxed, informal voice you use when you're so involved with what you're saying that you don't remember what you said—let alone how you said it.

CREATING A THIRD LANGUAGE

Colloquial language has vitality and vigor and gets to the point quickly with an informality that puts a reader at ease; but because it's used in the presence of a live listener, it often contains assumptions about common knowledge that don't translate well onto the page. ("It was really a trip," can mean a lot when you're describing a party to a friend. In a story, if this phrase is used as dialogue it can tell you a lot about character. But if it's a narrator's shorthand description of a party, it doesn't give readers any concrete images that help them see or hear the event.)

Literary language is more precise, takes time to focus on details, creates an atmosphere. Yet without the vigor of spoken language it becomes eviscerated. (Once I wrote a paragraph describing a character's trip to the bathroom. My language was archaic, abstract, and self-conscious. "What would you say if you were just talking?" a friend asked: "Oh, I'd just say: *He got up to pee*," I answered. "Why don't you try it here?" she asked. I thought I'd die before putting a phrase like that in a story. But when I followed her advice, it worked.)

When colloquial language unites with literary language, a third language often emerges—an alchemical blend of your natural speaking voice, and a more polished language capable of arousing the imagination of the reader. The more you write, the more this language occurs naturally, and the more your speaking and writing styles may begin to converge.

Learning about your natural speaking voice often involves a new kind of listening—just as you would listen to a foreign language. To get a grasp of colloquial voice, try listening to yourself in stores, on buses, with children, on the phone. As often as you can, write down what you hear yourself saying, using the words and phrases you choose naturally when you speak. If you speak simply, write simply. (Use "don't" instead of "do not," "they were supposed to be" instead of "they theoretically represented.") This may not be the language you'll end up using in your stories, and it certainly isn't the way you need to write all the time. But working this way can help you create a unique, natural amalgam of colloquial and literary speech.

Once you learn to listen to yourself, it's easier to listen to other people, and this leads naturally to an awareness of dialogue. You start to hear differences in speech patterns—the give-and-take in conversations. It sometimes helps to recall your linguistic origins: If your family spoke a dialect, mixed a foreign language with English, or spoke a foreign language at home, see if you can remember what they sounded like. (This is particularly important if your first language wasn't English.) Write at least one anecdote in an original language, or dialect, or say it out loud if you never learned to write in this language. There's no need to write a complicated story—you're simply trying to broaden the range of language, the way a singer practicing scales hits notes he or she may never sing.

Becoming aware of colloquial speech is helpful for another reason: It reminds you that every day you use language inventively. Remembering that you already know how to improvise when you speak can give you a kind of faith when you start to improvise in a story.

This kind of listening may lead you to discover that you're a writer who works, to some degree, in opposition to colloquial speech. You may find you work more naturally in the terrain of dreams, lyric imagery, surreal ideas—and the language of the street feels foreign to you. If this is the case, you'll still benefit by listening to the way you (and others) speak; but the emergence of your third language may require a different kind of work—for example, the kinds of exercises we suggested in the previous chapter, "Public and Private Voices."

The Chorus of Voice

As you begin to explore voice, you will undoubtedly begin to hear many voices speaking inside you. Some voices arise as if disembodied, offering mysterious sentences or phrases. *"Reset the turbo! Multiply!"* *"We can't be responsible."* *"If you don't have the money, you won't have the honey."* Others will be attached to characters, who begin to give hints about who they are. *"Chocolate is my God."* *"I don't trust anyone in a Panama hat."* Some will seem to start a story. *"On the first morning of May, Harold Springhouse arose to find every budding rose in his garden slashed from its stem."*

One of the most startling things about your inner voice may be its diversity. It's not one voice, but many. You've got a lot of company: voices that seem to come from nowhere, others that make return visits, some that have been chattering away for as long as you can remember.

It takes a while to get acquainted with these voices, to discover the ones you want to know, and those you wish never to hear from again. It takes a while, too, to understand how to work with these voices so they turn into stories: How to get characters to speak spontaneously, argue with each other, tell you why they have to speak. How to get phrases to unroll into whole paragraphs. How to entice narrators to disclose their tale.

Among those voices that roil with inner energy, that will take you somewhere, are voices that will lead to dead ends or curtail excitement—and learning to tell the difference doesn't happen immediately. A character will tell you his life story for fifty pages, then fizzle. A tongue-rolling phrase will delight you momentarily, but lead nowhere.

Sometimes, too, your sheer delight in voice can fool you. You may think you're speaking originally, when in fact you're borrowing a voice you've read or heard. You may feel you're tapping into exciting ideas, when the material is flat and lifeless. It takes a while to know how to handle this slippery aspect of voice.

When you open the door to voice, as with Pandora's Box, you're going to release all sorts of crazy creatures—ones that will plague and curse you along with those that give you hope. It's important not to have any misgivings. Let them all free. Remember, the voices that feel the most treacherous or untrustworthy often have the most potential. Give them a whole notebook. Let them dictate anytime they want to. Become their scribe. Later, you can be reckless. You can discard or destroy them. But not before you give them a chance to be fully themselves. If you cut your voice short too soon, you'll never discover what it can do.

The trick is to see potential in all of these voices. Milk them for whatever they have to offer, drape them in costumes, set them up in impossible circumstances. This is the way fiction writers must approach everything in the world. Your question should always be: What can I get from this person, this image, this situation?

A GALLERY OF ROGUES

1. Notice any voices that speak spontaneously inside you, any time of day or night. Write down what they say. Write a one-paragraph story using one of these voices.

2. Select one voice you've discovered. Imagine that voice as a character. What does this person look like? Sound like? Think about? Does he or she wear gloves? Glasses? Hats? Stand in front of the mirror and deliver a soliloquy as that character. Talk about the stock market. A favorite recipe. A secret love.

3. Imagine giving an enormous sum of money to three characters you've discovered in your head. How would each of them react? Now imagine making love to them.

4. Take two voices you've discovered that don't seem to belong to characters, and hear the rhythms of their speech. Notice their tone and energy. Is it acerbic? Languid? Lyric? Let them have a political argument in nonsense, capturing their tone and rhythms.

5. Select a voice that feels disturbing or unsettling and let it ramble as long as possible. Interview that voice for a job. Send it on a secret mission.

6. Take a voice on a walk with you.

Who's Speaking?: Voice and Character

As you play with the chorus of voices in your head, you'll undoubtedly discover characters—and something else as well. When it's linked to the imagination, voice is intimately connected to who you are, and it leaves you behind. You're sipping your cappuccino in a Berkeley café, wearing stone-washed jeans, but your story is narrated by a nineteenth-century wool spinner from Florence. Or your main character is a reclusive bookkeeper while you're a gregarious wine expert. A strange metamorphosis occurs: It's you speaking and not you speaking.

In the creation of characters, you're using your voice to project imaginatively into another body, perhaps another time and place. You're drawing on your emotions, memories, impressions, but you're throwing your voice—indeed your very self—like a ventriloquist. You're simultaneously being yourself (even discovering yourself!) and abandoning yourself to enter fully into the voice and body of another person. This is one of the extraordinary qualities of voice: its ability to clothe itself in the guise of being you *and* someone else.

The next time the voice of a character starts speaking inside you, pay attention. Write down everything this person has to say. If he seems to tire, urge him to keep talking. Ask for his life story. Ask what she most desires.

Notice how you relate to this character. Are you sitting in her presence, listening to her speak, watching her eat a bowl of cornflakes? Or do you seem to *become* this person, or to feel possessed by him? (Hint: later, this may give you a clue as to whether you'll write in the first or third person.) Practice with both. Listen to a character from the outside, as he packs a crate of oranges, complains about his wife. Then move inside his body. Feel the ache in his neck, his bent shoulders, the chill from the concrete floor. Smell the tart acid on your fingers. Become him, speak his words.

USING PERSONAE

One of the best ways to experience how you draw on yourself at the same time that you project onto a character is to play with persona voices. Personae are dramatic masks. They're aspects of yourself—sometimes hidden selves; sometimes your deepest, most fiery essence; sometimes a bland, surface quality—that you exaggerate and project onto a character. Your passionate judiciousness, your pickiness, your despair.

I have a persona voice that's always ready to speak when I let it: a Camille Paglia–style, rapid-fire, somewhat grating voice with opinions on everything from who serves the best cold salmon salad to why women shouldn't use tampons. I imagine this voice coming from a thirtyish woman who wears short black skirts and plastic banana earrings. The best part about her is that I don't have to take responsibility for anything she says. In the effort to be a reasonable, socially acceptable person in the world, I daily mute this strong part of myself. In my fiction, I can let my inner, opinionated self have a field day, with complete impunity. And I discover something else: What's fun and liberating for me is good for my stories.

Because they're exaggerated, persona voices have tremendous potential. They push a characteristic to the extreme, so they carry a charge. They're terribly disdainful, or bitterly sarcastic, or unrelentingly morose. You can hear their ranting long after they've left the room: "Harold, you idiot, I'm going to burn every page of that insipid manuscript!" They're not bland. Working with these persona voices is like mixing a strong drink: If you start with an ingredient that sizzles, your drink will be more likely to have a kick.

Persona voices can steer your plot in provocative directions, animate characters, and push a scene toward an edge that excites your reader. They also illuminate those parts of yourself that are a crucial part of your artistic signature, and let them glow like neon. With a wonderful sleight-of-hand, you become more fully yourself at the instant you disappear into your characters.

Some persona voices arise naturally, but you can also push yourself to discover new ones. To provoke them, try these improvisations. Invent others.

1. State one of your cherished beliefs (for example, "Women should be treated well" or "It's probably good not to sell your body for sex"). Speaking in the voice of someone who believes just the opposite, fulminate against this belief.

2. What retaliation fantasy have you had? Become a character who can carry out this fantasy (the female inventor of male birth control; a hippie named Rain who organizes antivivisectionist rallies), and describe the shocking details of a successful retaliatory plot.

3. Take on the voice of someone who lives in a very different world from your own (for example, the world of Washington politics, or beauty queens, or adding-machine salespeople). Reveal the most sordid details of your world.

4. What brutal fantasy do you harbor? What kind of person would act out that fantasy? Become that person and confess your exploits to the local tabloid.

5. What bland or superficial aspect of your personality do you detest? Become a character in whom this quality is exaggerated, and keep a journal of your daily conquests and obsessions.

6. When you were a teenager, what kind of friend would have appalled your parents? Write a short monologue in the voice of this unwelcome friend, telling your parents in detail what the two of you are going to do after dinner.

7. What kind of person has always both repelled and intrigued you? A serial killer who loves his cat? A hooker named Pearl who has an obsession with body hair? A bigot? A bully? Become this person. Take an imaginary walk down the main street in your town and editorialize vociferously on all the people you see along the way.

THE POWER OF CARICATURES

Sometimes there's no distinction between personae and characters. You hear a persona voice speaking—an authoritative, aggressive voice—and in an eye-blink that voice is a full-blown, dimensional character. He's phoning his corporate lawyers, plotting to liquidate a rival company. You can hear his commanding voice, see his slim fingers paging through manila files. Your plot is underway.

But personae can often present themselves initially as caricatures. You may resist surrendering to a voice that seems so flat or stereotyped or narrow. (How many times have you been warned to steer away from cardboard characters?!) Here's a secret about caricatures: If you trust your first instincts with these persona voices, and let even these cardboard characters speak, they'll begin to reveal their ambiguities and complexities. My Camille Paglia persona can easily get on your nerves after a while. She's unsympathetic and one-dimensional if all she does is rant. Yet I know there's more to her. I have to push myself to give her a quiet moment in a story, and see what feelings open up. I have to discover where she's vulnerable, what makes her sad.

The caricature is simply the early manifestation of the more intriguing and surprising person. Your persona voices will evolve. Like sea creatures moving up the evolutionary scale, they'll grow lungs, gain faith, an afterlife. They'll dangle a high heel, whisper their secrets. Perhaps they'll even surprise you by becoming unforgettable characters.

CHAPTER FOURTEEN

Capturing the Inner Critic

William James once called his brother, Henry James, "thin-blooded and priggish." So Henry created a character who had these characteristics.

— THE NEW YORK TIMES BOOK REVIEW

Whenever I ask students to say aloud what their inner critics tell them, the class becomes heated. Even the shyest writers, the ones who sit in the back row and rarely say a word, miraculously find their voice. "You can't write!" "Stop wasting your time!" "Don't you have better things to do?" "Who do you think you are?" "You haven't done enough research!"

Critics are angry and full of passion. Or cold and scathingly logical. Or lucid, ironic, elegant. They never lack for words. They capture your attention immediately. And you believe them.

These critic voices mingle with the chorus of other voices in your head. But unlike the voices that stimulate stories and lead to characters, critics try to direct your story from the outside. ("You don't know enough to write that story." "Your language is too ordinary.") They insist on their authoritative detachment—and it's this aloofness that gives them their power. When the voices speak, you hesitate. Maybe they're right. Your story stops, or you put it in the drawer.

As with any dark force, the way to disarm your critics is to make them work for you instead of against you—*use* their power rather than fight it. You want them to expend their energies inside your stories, not outside them. As Henry James knew well, critics are excellent sources for characters. As a voice outside your story, your English teacher instructing you to write logical paragraphs will stifle creativity. If you dress him in a derby hat, put a carnation in his lapel, and have him flirt with the French teacher at the races, in a terribly logical voice, he becomes a character—and propels your story forward.

Notice when your critic appears. At the peak of excitement about a story? The moment you've finished? Before you begin? Critics seem to have an uncanny instinct for interrupting at the most crucial moments in a story—moments for gathering momentum, making exciting leaps. Use these interruptions as opportunities to enlist your critic's anger, stubbornness, and ferocity. Channel that energy into your story. Or turn your critic into an ally who writes you a vociferous letter about why it's important to keep writing. Pin this letter above your desk.

"But what if the critic is right?" a student once asked, after a particularly hilarious recitation by the class's "critic" voices. She looked pained, and I had to concede: Sometimes the critic has good instincts. But instead of being a sympathetic ally, pushing you to a deeper level of the story, the critic makes you want to stop writing forever. Even when his observations contain truth, they have a cutting acerbic edge, a destructive, mocking undertone. The critic has a bad personality, harsh and unforgiving.

Over time, the discerning aspect of the critic may be absorbed by a sympathetic inner listener—the writer's ally. This is the good critic, who wants you to push your voice to its limits, finish your novel, sell it to a first-rate house and go on a ten-city book tour. This inner listener knows the deepest secrets of good writing: how to raise the hairs on your reader's arms. How to write a book they can't put down.

If your critic offers suggestions that energize you and make you want to write, then listen. Otherwise, don't hesitate to capture him or her! Describe his greatcoat. Inquire where she bought her umbrella. Let him write a true confession. Watch her cry at the opera. And if—like William James—he describes you in some unflattering way, turn that description into a character.

Learning to Spot the Imposter

*It would take a whole book to chart the brilliant deviations
the voice can take to prevent its owner from being known.*

— IRIS WARREN, VOICE TEACHER

As I write, I often think of Iris Warren, pacing the wooden floors
of her studio, listening intently to her singing students. An early
advocate of liberating the natural voice, she knew the difference
between voice as technique and voice connected to the heart,
between the voice of the throat and the voice of the whole body.
"False voice," Iris Warren said, "is noises that are born in the
throat and die just in front of the nose." Noises that may sound
pretty, may be executed with sophistication, but are not connected to one's inner spirit.

Writers, like singers, are often nervous performers. Relying
too heavily on technique, or craft, is just one of the many intri-
cate ways writers disguise themselves from themselves, and from
the world. A whole cast of other imposter voices waits in the
wings to step in when the writer is feeling uncomfortable. The
academic voice, the psychological voice, the literary voice.
The voice of abstraction and analysis, the overly logical voice,
the polite voice. You write "His words set off defensive signals
in my mind" instead of "I was furious."

These imposter voices are essentially "head" voices. They

have important uses in other parts of your life. You need them when you're giving a report to the Board of Directors, explaining why your bank balance is wrong, or facing an irate mother-in-law. As the voice that drives your story, though, they'll lead you astray. Think of the voice of psychologists or "active listening" advocates: "What I hear you saying is. . . . " It's great for saving marriages and helping us survive our teenagers' parties, but its fairness and detachment is deadly for writers.

Because they're developed for specific, usually practical uses, imposter voices have a limited range. They can't stand up to the demands of the creative imagination that needs a wide, open sky. And they're not connected to the heart, but have a cunningly constructed plumbing all of their own, a direct line from the head to the mouth, circumventing the organs, bypassing the gut. As a result, these imposter voices are colorless, anemic. They don't convey tone, or a distinctive authorial presence.

Sometimes your imposter voice is simply a way that you write before you tap the honesty of a deeper part of yourself, before you learn to bring your inner energy into your writing. The more you work, the more your imposter voice will fade, and you'll discover yourself saying things directly, cutting through layers of practiced politeness, posturing, or abstractness.

It may also be the case that your imposter voice is a response to your inner critic. Your critic voice tells you you can't write, so you embellish your sentences with beautiful phrases, carefully culled words. Yet as you prove to your critic that you can write impressive sentences, you move away from the voice that's connected to your heart and feelings.

Getting rid of your imposter voice may depend on silencing your critic. Tell him/her you're okay the way you are. You don't need to use fancier language, be more intellectual, more this, more that, to be a good writer. You can speak simply, from the heart.

L I S T E N I N G   F O R   T H E   I M P O S T E R

Training your ear to hear the difference between writing that is alive and writing that isn't is one of your greatest challenges in working with voice. You began to do this with the exercise in Chapter Seven, "Distilling Voice," where you read something you wrote aloud and responded from your gut to those passages that felt charged. The best way to hear yourself is to literally listen to your own voice. Read your work aloud regularly. Pace the room as you read. Feel the language in your body. Have someone else read your work to you. Or tape record yourself as you read, then listen to yourself.

The more you do this, the more you'll hear those shifts in your voice—from sensory to interpretive, from direct to decorative, from colloquial to cerebral—those places where the imposter appears. Listen for shifts in diction, in emotional energy. Notice the places where your language becomes abstracted or interpretive, where you explain or justify, where you resort to pretty language rather than plunge into emotion, where you veer away from a tense or risky moment. The voice of your story doesn't short-circuit at crucial moments, but says just what you mean, in language that is your own.

It's also useful to read aloud from a writer whose work you admire. Feel the rhythms, the sensory language, the direct presentation of feelings.

F O I L I N G   T H E   I M P O S T E R

You can foil the imposter by parodying your own tendencies. If, when writing a scene, you tend to analyze or explain the dramatic action, write deliberately in psychological jargon, or as a pedantic professor. If you find that you sometimes write romantic, overblown description, write as a hyperbolic tour guide. By exaggerating, you amplify your imposter voice, making it easier to hear.

As you do this, you may discover something exciting: Imposters, like critics, can make dazzling debuts as characters. Your repertoire of imposter voices is like the costume room of a theater. In there you'll find the vague, philosophical New-Ager, the arcane Freudian, the detached, abstract hermeneutics graduate student. Let these characters flaunt and strut, speak unabashedly, and you'll stumble on some four-star actors. Even the imposter voice that is reticent and elliptical, unable to talk about what is important, can make a noteworthy character: think of Chauncy Gardner in *Being There* by Jerzy Kosinski.

Unlike singers, writers can make use of voices that are thin, colorless, or off-key. By giving your imposter voices a place to live and room to maneuver, you'll not only create some marvelous characters, you'll find your story itself takes on a new life.

Here are some other imposter antidotes.

For attacks of unrelenting intellectual analysis and psychologizing:

1. Tell your story (or a passage of your novel) in the voice of a child. Use only the language of the senses. Now write the story or passage in the voice of an adult, still using only the language of the senses.

2. Go back to Chapter Five and repeat the exercise on pages 17–19, in which you write as if you're speaking from a part of your body. Take a passage from your story or novel that sounds like it's written by a "head" voice, and rewrite it imagining your voice is coming from your diaphragm, or your gut, or your heart.

For treatment of politeness, tact, or faintness of heart:

1. Invent a persona voice for a person who is outspoken, unconcerned about what others think of her, even abrasive. Let her dictate a story.

    2. Take a minor character from one of your stories, a character whose voice has been sidelined but who you think may have more to say, and make him/her a main character in a short story.

    3. Invent a character who is timid and demure. Invent another character who is nervy and a bit brash. Let them talk to each other about writing. About their fathers. About their greatest fear.

    4. Focus on the event, person, or image that has been most damaging, upsetting, and scalding in your life and write about it in detail.

For impulses to beautify and impress:

    1. Take a story that you've written and retell it, speaking aloud. Don't read from the page. Simply tell the story to a real or imaginary listener in your natural voice. Tape record yourself as you speak. Compare your oral delivery with the story on the page.

    2. Go through a story you've written and remove all adjectives and adverbs. Read the story aloud and hear the difference.

Invent your own antidotes to fit your personal imposter!

The Writer as Presence

I want to hear you, not your voice.

—IRIS WARREN,
VOICE TEACHER

When I first began to write seriously, I was enthralled with Donald Barthelme. I memorized paragraphs of his stories and his syntax infused my dreams. One day I got a rejection letter from an editor that said: "Your stories are perfect imitations of Donald Barthelme—I would even go so far as to say they are brilliant imitations. However, you have effaced so much of yourself and hidden away your passions so carefully, there is nothing left of yourself. . . . "

This letter confronted me with the fact that I would have to learn to work with who I was. My imitation of Barthelme was perfect, even brilliant. But I hadn't fooled a good editor. My own presence, that spirit that gives rise to voice, had been missing from my stories. My work was haunted by Donald Barthelme's ghost.

Most writers feel compelled to write because they want to put some part of themselves into their work, something that gives unique and artistic expression to who they are. They want, on some level, to introduce themselves to the reader. But since no writer has actually written much when this longing first arises, it's usually accompanied by abstract preconceptions, even romantic ideas about the relationship between identity and art. When most writers start to write, they do exactly what I did: They infuse their stories with the writer they'd like to be, rather than the writer they're afraid they really are—a writer who doesn't have much to write, or, even if she does, won't say it with much eloquence.

As we will discuss in the next chapter, there's value to imitation. Barthelme's voice had allowed me to take certain risks with my imagination and the way I used language—risks that might even lead me to the writer I really was. However, the relationship between artistic projection and identity is complicated. Like Barthelme, I might choose to veil much of my life in metaphor; yet allowing my own presence to expand fully was still crucial to releasing my voice. This is true for all writers: At the very moment you disappear into your story, you must still be right there, working with who you are.

Once I was disabused of transforming myself into Donald Barthelme, I began to work more honestly with myself. I didn't do anything special. I just surrendered to the fact that all I'd ever have to work with was my own quality of presence. Since my stories no longer glistened with Barthelme's imaginary aura, they felt quite ordinary to me. But other people didn't find them so. There was another surprise as well: When I read some of my stories over, I discovered something new in them—a way of seeing the world I'd always had, long before I'd read Donald Barthelme or Flannery O'Connor or Jane Austen, or any other writer. One might say that I was beginning to articulate my vision and see it reflected in my work.

Most writers are highly aware of the way other writers infuse their work with themselves. When you read a good novel or a story, you leave with the sense that—in addition to having met particular characters and having entered a particular world—you've met a particular writer. Whether the story is written in the first person or the third, with a chatty, personal narrator or an impersonal one, it's pervaded by a definite presence. Even nineteenth-century writers, who often wrote in the voice of an omniscient narrator, imbued their fiction with a highly personal stamp: The presence behind the story that Nathaniel Hawthorne creates is distinct from that of Emily Brontë.

What you often don't realize is that you also have a unique presence. In fact every person does, and you can learn to project it in your work—simply by getting out of your own way. This quality is a central aspect of your voice, and like voice itself, it's in some ways quite simple. It's everything you bring to your experience at that moment (including your vision, your imagination, your quirks of personality, your memories, your sense of language, your impatience, your ability to experience people). You may never sing one autobiographical note. You may never utter one personal fact about your history. But you are stuck with being a particular person with a particular past, writing on a particular day, and some essential part of you is going to escape into what you write: Writing is an inevitably and effortlessly self-revealing act.

This realization can be a turning point for writers—both in freeing voice and finding material. What emerges is a sense of willingness to work with whatever you are, the sheer ordinariness and uniqueness of your being. You may mute some surface elements of personality (a tendency to be overly logical or earnest) that get in the way of your voice. And you may also exaggerate elements (the same tendency to be logical, a highly ironic sense of humor) for dramatic effect. You may create personae. But it's important not to back away from letting your most honest self infuse your story.

You don't have to be comfortable with who you are to let your presence suffuse your writing, nor do you have to know yourself in the sense of being psychologically sophisticated. But you do have to be honest with yourself and your own sense of language and storytelling.

Take some time to experience your body as you write. Listen to your breath. Notice your hands, legs, arms, feet. And once—

just once—put a mirror near your desk. See who is actually writing.

Identify some quality or quirk that you don't like about yourself. Write a story in which this quality dominates. Find humor, absurdity, in this trait.

Write a story about a person from another culture (or another planet) who meets you for the first time. Write from the other person's point of view. Make your story funny, poignant, sad.

After you've written even one story, you can begin to work concretely with the way your presence impacts your work. You can ask yourself whether you feel an authentic connection to the material. Does this feel like *your* story, and no one else's? Have you packaged your presence to make it presentable? Have you muted it out of fear? Depending on your answers, you can reflect back and dig deeper, or take a breath and keep going. This is why it's important to finish stories, or a novel. Any collection of work, even if small, and even if it disappoints you, allows you to relate to the larger issue of how you—the whole person— inform your writing. If your presence has been muffled in a particular story, it's still useful to have written it and be able to recognize what's missing. Even when they're not successful, your stories are a testing ground for voice, an honest gauge of your artistic projection at the moment.

Letting your fullest, most powerful presence pervade your writing requires courage. It also requires an attitude of curiosity and receptivity that allows you to weave in and out of experiencing your life and detaching from it long enough to notice it. This isn't the clinical detachment of the scientist. It's the passionate, lively detachment of a writer.

Becoming a Prose Thief

Every writer knows what imitation feels like: how easy it is after reading a whole slew of nineteenth-century writers to write as if you're standing behind a podium. Words like "whilst" and "nary" spring into your prose, unbidden. Or how reading Raymond Carver makes you want to write in a chummy, over-a-beer voice, with characters who say "So anyway," and "Well, hell." You can have great fun writing in these voices; the words and ideas may tumble out easily. Characters prance and sidle, fights break out, insights leap onto the page. But ultimately you'll become uneasy. Where's the voice that's your own?

In your search for the voice that tells stories in your own way, you'll likely spend time trying on other voices—seeing how they fit, parodying them, changing them around. These influences are essential. No writer creates in a vacuum. Whatever rhythms or styles you're drawn to—formality or informality, lyric gracefulness or clipped ennui, effusive description or stark, minimalist utterings—try them on for size. But don't stop there.

The key to keeping these other voices from obscuring your own is to be bold, even ruthless. Remember this: *Bad writers borrow; good writers steal.* Don't settle for halfway measures. When you borrow a voice, you take it as it is. Like a coat that's too large, the effect looks borrowed. When you make the influence your own, you don't hesitate to make alterations. You shape it to fit you, putting it through the filter of your world view, your way of talking, your sense of rhythm. Alice Walker says the easy, loping grace of Zora Neale Hurston's folktales pulses through her as she writes. But you'd never mistake Walker's voice for Hurston's. She's taken in Hurston's stories like nourishment, until they're in her blood and bones.

Here are some exercises to develop your bravado as a prose thief:

1. Select a passage from one of your least favorite writers. Appoint yourself as artistic director. How would you do the scene differently? Change the intention of the scene, or the tone. Shift the angle of vision. Redefine the characters.

2. Narrate a short incident in the voice of your favorite author. Parody and exaggerate the voice. See whether you discover anything about the incident that you hadn't known before.

3. Rewrite the incident again, in the voice of another, very different writer. Veer across the spectrum, from the spare lyricism of Amy Tan, to the cerebral intensity of Don DeLillo. Does the tone change? The details of incident?

4. Create a two-way correspondence between yourself and a writer you admire. Steal the persona of your admired writer as you write back to yourself: Write the way you think he or she would talk. Write to dead writers as well as ones still alive. Tell them why you like their writing. Invent their response.

5. Correspond in the same way with a writer who irritates you, a writer you despise.

Playing with the voice of another writer serves important purposes. It can lead you to the characters, events, and themes you want to write about. A student wrote a story imitating Grace Paley's voice, and found himself writing about a young man searching for the father he'd never known. He filtered his story through the gutsy, gum-smacking voice he knew from Grace Paley's writing, but this imitation led him to his own inner material—a powerful drive to conjure up an absent father.

Seizing the voice of another writer can also help you feel permission to write about something you might otherwise have backed away from. (If Jamaica Kincaid can write about the intense mother-daughter bonds during childhood and puberty, why can't you?) It can help you feel the wide range of possibility in the way a story can be told: in the use of language, syntax, narration, how events unfold, how the writer engages the reader. Or it can be the warm-up that leads to your story, the exercise that gets you in tone so your voice can take over.

Using the Journal Dangerously

DIARY COWS

Got up early, waited for the farmer.
He hooked us all to the machines as
usual. Typical trip to the pasture,
typical day grazing and ruminating.
About 5:00 back to the machines. What
relief! Listened to the radio
during dinner. Lights out at 7:00.
More tomorrow.

—RONALD KOERTGE

One place our private voice goes when we're an adult is into our journal. Here we unburden, kevetch, take leaps of fantasy, talk from the heart, say things we wouldn't say out loud. Recently, I looked back over some of my journals from years ago. Doing this is always a rather bizarre, out-of-body experience, like floating on the ceiling and viewing, below, a person that is both you and strangely distant. But I was thinking about voice, and I realized something: Talking privately, from the heart, isn't always the same as finding your voice.

I've used my journals, as we all do, in many ways—as a place to lodge that reassuring list of daily events: *Took Lisa to her school Halloween parade. She looked adorable in her green tutu and speckled face paint.* As a place for comfort—confiding as I would to a friend. As a place to think, to record random thoughts and abstract musings. Reading through these entries, I saw flashes of original ideas, occasional jolting images, but for the most part I saw that I'd used my journal as a safety valve, not a pressure cooker. I'd used easy, bland language, or the language of the head. Comfortable language. Imposter language. The emotions were heartfelt, but I wasn't pushing myself into the terrain of raw voice, with its unaccountable images, those words that fly out of nowhere.

I saw something else, too. My journal voice was a confidential one, unconcerned with audience. Sometimes I wrote in a personal shorthand that released for me a store of memories— a dinner with my sister I'd forgotten about, when she told me about the break-up of her marriage. Reading, I'm taken back to that fall evening, her fingers pushing back her hair, our ragged conversation. What I feel, though, is triggered by my internal memories. The scenes and details are in my mind, not on the page. Another reader wouldn't feel the spark of emotion I do. She would see only a half-revealed moment. To write for a reader, I'd need to flesh out the abbreviations, translate the shorthand into scenes and concrete images.

Only when I used my journal as a transport area for phrases, dreams, or images that I didn't try to organize or understand, did I see those unmistakable shards of raw voice, waiting for me to return to them. *Carried his father on his back. Radio love. This is as far as we know to go.*

M A K I N G   T H E
J O U R N A L   D A N G E R O U S

The trick to using the journal as a testing ground for voice is simple: You must allow it to be dangerous. Use it to discover what you don't yet know about yourself and your life rather than to record what you already do know. Use it to discover language that is unrefined, shot from the gut. Here you can experiment freely, without fear of observation, scavenge your life, develop audacity.

The following exercise is an alternative to the usual daily log. At the end of your day, take some time to be alone and remember what happened. Stay away from the official version of your day (what you'd tell someone who asked: "What did you do?") and concentrate on images and events that stick with you. You may remember excited voices at a street fair, the red flash of a colleague's coat, your child's sulky "good-bye" as he leaves for school. And you may forget things that you imagined were important, like finishing a report, meeting a friend for lunch. What you do remember may not be something that you think is relevant to your life. But it will often have emotional significance and suggest other events or images, even scenes.

For example, if you asked me what I did today, I'd probably say: "I got up in the morning and went right down to my studio and wrote nonstop for the entire day, except for watering the garden and eating a few crackers. In the evening I went out at about nine o'clock for dinner by myself because my husband was working late and my son was at sleep-away camp. Then I came home, worked some more, talked to my husband and went to bed."

This is all true; but if I allow my mind to drift, this is what I remember: the muddy look of reheated coffee in a saucepan early in the morning, white sheets on a neighbor's clothesline. Hours later I see myself in the bank—an event I forgot when I told you my official version. My shoulder bag is pulling on the left sleeve of my T-shirt and I'm tugging at the sleeve, hoping the teller won't notice. When it's my turn to go to the teller he winks, making me wonder whether the wink has anything to do with the sleeve. I also remember the way a baked potato looked at dinner—white baked potato softened by candlelight.

Both are reports of the same day. Both are accurate. But the first version is schematic, and the second takes me right back into parts of my day. Indeed, if I compare spontaneous images with the "official report" of my day, I feel the difference between writing about events because they have emotional and visceral significance—and writing about events merely because they happened. None of these images are particularly profound—in fact, most are rather trivial. But often such images lead to parts of myself I don't know about (ambivalence about being sexual, for example, more interest in the appearance of food than I'm aware of). This sort of awareness can alert me to a deeper resonance below seemingly trivial images. It also leads me to a keener awareness of myself in general—an awareness that keeps me honest and helps me key into material.

If you begin to keep this kind of journal, it's good to reread it occasionally. Sometimes one or two elements excite you, trigger short paragraphs, a new freewrite, even a story. You also begin to learn what matters to you—what kinds of people you notice, what conversations you remember, what events are magnetic for you. And this helps sharpen your writer's ear and writer's eye. Some detail you've written about earlier may surface when you're writing a story—right when you need it. You may also find yourself transforming those daily lists of events into zany personal commentary, as Ronald Koertge's diary cows did. The mundane is no longer mundane.

There will be times when you'll want to abandon experimentation and return to the sheer comfort of the journal as a place to confide, without any regard for style or content, just the way you'd return to a comfortable couch and a cup of tea. After you've used the journal as a place to stretch your voice, this highly personal journal may also deepen.

Writing in the Pressure Cooker: Leading Raw Voice into the Story

Sitting in the dark of Gregory's room, with a cigar in his hand and Glenn Miller playing "Chattanooga Choo-Choo" softly beside him, Jerome began a bunny story. "Once upon a time, there was a bunny who lived with his mommy and daddy in a bunny hole at the edge of the great green wood." All the other bunny stories started with that sentence. After it, Jerome was deep in the terror of fictional improvisation.

— CHARLES BAXTER,
FROM *THE WOULD-BE FATHER*

Improvisation is an inescapable reality of fiction. That wonderful, scary freefall into improvisation through freewrites and spontaneous jottings is where voice begins. Once you've got something on the page, you move into a second-order improvisation: You start improvising with the found objects your voice has offered. These objects may be simple: an image of a man peering into a refrigerator; a phrase, *Once upon a time there was a bunny*. Or they may be complex: a schematic idea for a plot, a list of questions that haunt you. Whatever they are, to move your voice into a story, you have to make a commitment to working with certain found elements.

Often your voice can make this transition easily. A story gets written as if you're taking dictation, one element leading to another. At other times, you may clutch at this point, lose the freedom and energy of beginnings. You worry that those first, inspired images or lines won't lead you anywhere. You wish you hadn't caught that man looking into the refrigerator. You're sorry that first line about the bunny ever occurred to you.

If the commitment to certain specific elements (a character, a turn of events) freezes your voice, remember you don't have to keep this commitment forever. You may end up with material for a different story than the one you intended to write. Or the elements you're working with may never quite coalesce and you may have to put the story aside. But you'll never discover what these objects can do unless you commit to working with them.

Remember, too, that your natural voice improvises all the time—just like the three-year-old in Chapter Nine who told the story about the lamp and the pig. Intuitively, she knew that she had made a commitment to the pig by using him to start her story. So when her attention was distracted by the lamp, she didn't forget the pig—on the contrary she had him propose to the lamp. She understood she had to do two rather contradictory things to tell her story: stay focused on certain constant elements, and let her voice be loose, inventive. She didn't tell a sophisticated story. But she made an excellent leap into second-order improvisation—that improvisation that happens when you're focusing on certain found elements of your story.

W R I T I N G   I N   T H E
P R E S S U R E   C O O K E R

If you paint a landscape with only two colors, you'll really find out what those two colors can do. Similarly, when writing, if you focus on two or three elements—the smoke over a charred field, a child sitting on a burnt tire drinking from a jar of water—you'll discover where they can lead you. Limitations, like a deadline, can push you in good ways.

1. Go back to a freewriting exercise or journal entry and pick out three significant images or events. Use these as the basis for a story which takes place in a five-minute period.

2. Choose two characters that have been speaking in your head or that appeared in a freewrite exercise. Put them in one setting. Give them a conflict that they have to solve in a single hour. The conflict can be seemingly trivial (which movie to see), or more dramatic (whether to rob a bank). Write a story that takes place within these limits.

3. Write a story about a person walking along a path. The whole story has to take place in one hour, and the person can't leave the path.

These new limits you're working with are an essential pressure cooker for your material, a tension that opens up opportunity. When you unleash your improvisational energies inside a container, they're more explosive. You've lost a blank drawing board, but you've gained the life force of the objects you've found. If you let them, these objects will crack open, expand.

If

If acts as a lever to lift us out of the world of actuality into the realm of imagination.

— KONSTANTIN STANISLAVSKY

If is an improvisational tool that can help your voice stay loose and inventive, at the same time that it leads you deeper into your story. Stanislavsky, the famous Russian director, says the power of *if* comes from two things. First, we know that what *if* suggests is a supposition, not real. *If* lets us accept this unreality freely, with confidence. Second, *if* arouses action. When you start with an *if*, action has to follow. "*If* a gardener digs up an old vase on an estate while he's working. . . ." The gardener's hands are in the dirt. He's looking nervously over his shoulder.

The imaginative motor that *if* provides can launch your story. It's also a force that can keep your story going, or jump-start it when it lags. From the first *if* arise others. "*If* the gardener takes the vase home and hides it . . . " or "*if* another gardener, whom he has a crush on, walks by as he finds the vase. . . . " *If* gives your voice direction, and energy.

Begin with this sentence:

If a young woman knocks on the door of her ex-boyfriend's apartment, a man she hasn't seen in two years . . .

Add another:

If he answers, looking distracted, the phone held to his ear . . .

Add another:

If she has left her job and is out of money . . .

Add three more *ifs* . . .

Now start writing. Whenever you feel stuck use a few more *ifs* to get your voice going.

Try this exercise with your own set of found objects—those images or characters that your raw voice has discovered. See where they take you.

If is an expansive force. It can provide the push you need by freeing you from a dependence on memory, or an actual event. You may begin writing about a character or place you know well, and then end up feeling constrained by the literal. (You're writing a story about Uncle Jack, but don't remember what happened after he broke his arm, so the story stops.) *If* lets you leave the familiar behind, shake loose from the control of the known. It helps you lead the outpourings of raw voice into a voice that can tell a story.

Story

CHAPTER TWENTY-ONE

Craft and the Voice of the Story

Many writers tell a story first, and learn about craft later. I know
I did: One of my first complete stories was triggered by something I'd read in the paper about a village in the northeast that
created a communal compost heap in the town square. The story
triggered graphic images of coffee grounds, bacon, soggy Cheer-
ios, cantaloupe seeds—all heaped around a statue of a general.
I began to describe the garbage, and soon the village came alive
for me. Each scene triggered the next with a sense of inevitable
logic. Characters spoke, complications occurred, and the garbage transformed into a glowing tree. "I've found my voice!" I
thought, when I finished the story. "This is it. Now I can write
stories forever."

Yet soon I was back to staring at fragments. Had my muse
tricked me? He'd shown me that intuitively I could organize
elements of voice into a whole story, but he hadn't explained
what I needed to know in order to do it again. Now, of course,
I was seduced. I *wanted* to do it again. For a long time, I did a
lot of floundering.

I read about other writers. I tried writing in the third person, the first person, the second person. I experimented with dialogue, and flip-flopped between the present and past tense. One day, inspired by an article I'd read about Gogol's short-lived teaching career at the University of St. Petersburg, I wrote a very short story called "Gogol's Class." As the story starts, Gogol's students are waiting for him to appear, and complaining bitterly. When Gogol arrives thirty minutes late—looking elegant in his black boots—he's holding an umbrella in one hand and a roast chicken in the other. Brushing aside complaints, he places the chicken on the podium and announces that he wants to sell it: The students leap to their feet, scavenging their pockets for rubles.

This wasn't a long story. But I'd written it with less trial and error. For one thing, I'd grown more familiar with a certain kind of detached third-person narrator—a narrator I'd met by accident in earlier stories—and I was more willing to follow her intuitive leaps. I was also beginning to trust that certain paths (in my case dialogue) led deeper into my story and understand that others (in my case an abundance of lyric imagery) led further away. The outcome of my story still surprised me. But some of what I'd done to achieve the outcome was less of a surprise.

Between these two stories, I'd begun to find a way to think about my own fiction. I'd begun to mull over questions like the narrator's role, the story's pace, use of dialogue, point of view, and tension. These terms weren't abstract to me. I'd identified them by learning the patterns of my own voice and experimenting with these patterns in shaping stories.

This is very important to remember. You can learn the concepts of craft by taking classes and reading books. But you won't know how to work with them and they won't have concrete meaning unless you discover them in the outpourings of your own voice. This is because the craft of fiction wasn't invented by critics and teachers. It comes from stories and the voices that create them. When the first stories were told, there were no words like "dialogue," "character," "plot," and "tension."

People simply told stories and other people listened. Later, when stories began to be written down, terms referring to craft entered the language. These terms are useful. But they're always recipes after the fact, and even today you rarely find the word "character" in most stories—anymore than you taste pure yeast in a loaf of bread. If you treat craft as a recipe, the fire of raw voice goes out. Our purpose in this section is to give you some techniques that help you experiment with craft and keep the fire alive.

The best way to tell a story that is yours and no one else's is to stay connected to the spontaneous forms that raw voice takes. You can learn to recognize potential characters, flesh out dialogue, develop tension. You can also get better at improvising, as well as knowing when to manipulate voice. But even in your final story, many of the phrases, images, and characters appear exactly as you first wrote them in spontaneous freewrites or scribbled notes. The voice that finally tells a story is nothing special. It's simply the final organization of raw voice into a form. It's what is left when everything that isn't essential is stripped away.

A polished writer's voice isn't a static commodity waiting for you in a drawer. It's the result of raw voice working through the story, refining itself, finding ways to gather momentum, creating images that reverberate within a larger context. You won't find it at the National Bureau of Standards. It changes with each story and is newly discovered with every act of writing.

As you learn to weave back and forth between loss of control and more conscious manipulation of voice, your raw voice will change, broaden its range. Skills of craft—like grounding scenes in concrete details, varying action with dialogue—become so automatic you do them without thinking.

A surprise also occurs: The more skilled you become at writing a story, the more voice has a way of disappearing. Your voice becomes part of the content of the story, assumes the voices of characters, dissolves into the voice of the omniscient narrator, loses itself in a description of a place. By the time the story is finished, you no longer have a sense of exactly "where" voice is. It has disappeared into the story itself. By the end of this section, we hope you will have lost track of your voice at least once, and told an entire story.

CHAPTER TWENTY-TWO

Going Deeper into the Story: Voice as Composer and Instrumentalist

In the beginning there was chaos. Then God took a breath and the world began.

— CREATION MYTH FROM THE *KABBALAH*

Writers often get a glimpse of what it feels like to play God. Your first words and ideas can issue forth magically, charged with primal energy, settling into the vague shape of a world: A woman gets off a train in Kansas City. She rummages in her purse, finds several unmailed letters, the address of a boarding house. She looks worried, she's obviously a stranger. And now a man in a dark coat hurries over, hands her his card, and walks away.

I see this woman clearly: She's dark-haired, fair-skinned, wears a vintage velvet jacket, and carries a duffel bag with the word *Belfast* stitched on it in blue letters. But there are a lot of other things about her I don't know. What is she doing in Kansas City? What will become of the unmailed letters? As I become a detective in my own story, all sorts of questions come up.

In some ways, it's more fun to be God. The initial burst of energy that heralds a story can feel like pure spontaneous combustion. You invent a treasure hunt off the coast of Bali; an anorexic dancer cuts a tendon while walking barefoot along the beach. But once you've set down these spontaneous lines and images—the dash to the hospital, the doctor who tells her she may never dance again—you inherit a fact-strewn landscape and have to walk more carefully through your own story. Now leaps of imagination (the kind that come so easily in freewriting) are tethered to the objects of a world you've begun to shape. This requires spontaneity of a different order. You have to channel inspiration into form.

How I hold onto the levity of my first images as I settle this woman into the dusty streets of Kansas City depends on my ability to work with these first-found objects while going deeper into the heart of the story. This is where spontaneous voice and considerations of craft converge. And this is where the music of voice begins to work with a new aspect of patterning.

VOICE AS A COMPOSER
AND AN INSTRUMENTALIST

In the first section of this book, we compared raw voice to a musical instrument, or a solo singer. Like a single instrument, raw voice manifests in specific instances and initially doesn't have to worry about how it fits into a pattern. The character's scarf is *vermilion,* not red. A polite librarian blurts out, *I don't give a damn.* As you start to work with raw voice you often experience an exhilarating sense of freedom.

But when you write a whole story or a novel, part of your voice works more like a composer—or a jazz musician creating an entire piece. This aspect of voice is guided by long-range concerns as well as by the spontaneous instincts of raw voice. Sometimes the composer gives raw voice free reign. Sometimes it restricts voice to work with previous elements. Over time, as you write, you get better at making choices that lead to the heart of your story: you're launched in a story and seem to pull something from midair (what we called "making something up" when we were kids). This often feels completely spontaneous. Yet you're probably relying on learned patterns and hours of practice, as well as inspiration—just like a composer who writes a piece in a single sitting, or a jazz musician who performs an extraordinary riff.

You may be the kind of writer who makes choices intuitively, or you may create elaborate plot sheets. You may, at various times, do both. But no matter how you work, you have to make choices in the process of creating a story—choices that give your story coherent form and lead to its completion. Your voice is unique. There are no fixed rules. You have to discover your own patterns and use them to forge a story's shape.

In this phase of creativity, voice engages in a more complex kind of orchestration. It emerges as the teller of a complete story—the composer of an entire piece. It also fragments into individual phrases, sentences, voices of characters, narrators— separate instruments or soloists. There are no exercise books for the well-tempered novel, no arpeggios for compelling dialogue. All writers must learn to work with this cacophony in their own way.

From Anecdotes to Stories

Many first stories start as short descriptions about your life and often contain a certain sense of potential. Did you ever tell someone an anecdote—perhaps something that's happened to someone you know—and have them say, "You have to write that down!" You follow their advice but are disappointed with the results. The story feels flat. An interesting event in life hasn't translated onto the page—even though you've told it faithfully.

You may have written the anecdote *too* faithfully and haven't yet figured out how to turn it into a story. You may also have told it with very few details, using a sketchy shorthand code, expecting the listener or reader to translate the events. An anecdote *is* an interesting linear sequence of events. There's an implicit tension between the speaker and the story in these circumstances. The speaker functions as both a narrator and a character—living in both the *now* of the storytelling and the *then* of the events within the story (if only as an eyewitness). When the circumstances are right, the listener has an immediate, direct experience of the speaker, and transmits this experience to the events. But the moment the live speaker vanishes, the tension vanishes too. The anecdote becomes a flat chronology, without contrasts. And the first-person narrator of the story vanishes as a vivid person, or what we might call a "found," fully embodied character in the story.

An anecdote is an engaging moment, made more engaging by the speaker. But it's a slender incident, with no complex level of meaning. Often you can summarize its message, like the moral of a fable. The anecdote about Bill who got a stomachache from eating all the watermelon at the family picnic (so his cousin Nathan couldn't eat it first) may translate into the moral: Gluttony doesn't pay. The anecdote is easily reduced to a one-sentence lesson—and it's often revived because of this lesson. Every time someone in Bill's family eats too much turkey or strawberry pie the anecdote is handed up (and perhaps embellished further) amid much laughter one more time.

A story, though, can't be reduced without destroying it. It needs life beyond its personal or entertainment value. It must be expansive, reverberating with layers of meaning and significance that will be important to a stranger who doesn't know the principal characters at all. It's larger than a one-sentence quip.

In order to transform an anecdote into a full-blown narrative you have to find the hidden story, something that erupts within and provides momentum and tension. This often requires invention, embellishment. It also requires working with your voice, so you know your own personal sense of a story. On the page you have to torque and twist the anecdote to get it to convey what it instantly conveyed when told out loud. This is a strange and paradoxical kind of deception, which brings the reader closer to the truth.

You also have to work with the narrator of the story. If the story had its roots in an anecdote about yourself, you now have to remember that the first-person narrator has slipped into a fictional world, and become a character. When you told your family story about Bill to a friend you were right in front of her. She could see your face, hear inflections of your voice, see your gestures. On the written page, however, a first-person narrator is a blank slate until he is dramatized, fleshed-out, and given a distinct voice. We'll talk more about this in Chapter Twenty-seven, "Meeting the First-Person Narrator."

WORKING WITH ANECDOTES

If you're clear on the character and voice of the narrator, it often doesn't take much to turn an anecdote into a story. Something as simple as finding a small image can make the events reverberate, give actions layers of meaning.

I once wanted to tell a story about a family going on a car trip from the point of view of a fourteen-year-old girl. The family—an extremely histrionic and disorganized family—set off on the trip late at night, against the advice of friends. As they drove through towns where all the motels were filled, the parents began to argue violently. At some point the mother opened the door of the car, threatened to jump out, and the father pulled the car over to the side of the road. As I thought about this story, I was sure I had a sequence of events and a clear sense of characters. But I didn't have a sense of what my story was moving toward, nor could I feel any tension or universal resonance: It seemed like a flat description of a disaster. Then one day I was reading a story in the newspaper about a nuclear plant in the desert. I had a vivid image of the wide-open spaces in the desert, the nuclear plant interestingly erased. As I was daydreaming about those spaces, I felt the emptiness of the desert as a sensation in my body. I felt sad, adventurous, excited, lonely, as though I were right in the middle of that flat, hot land. Without reaching for language, I heard the voice of the girl say: *"My mother then shouted that she was really leaving and opened the door so wide I could see the whole midwest—ordinary, frightening, far too real for the likes of us. . . ."*

When I heard this sequence, I knew I had my story. At the time this was purely intuitive knowledge, although in retrospect, I can tell you why: The girl's glimpse of the midwest transformed her mother's act from something purely violent into a poignant desire to escape. In that glimpse, the girl saw her own ambivalent feelings about the world beyond the car, a world that was frightening, almost numinous in its matter-of-fact reality, far too real for the family. In that moment the mother and daughter were both close and very separate. I'd found my hidden story.

To work with turning an anecdote into a story try these exercises:

1. Remember an event that your family told over and over again, and try to choose something that you either found extremely funny or embarrassing. Now ask yourself: Was it an anecdote? Or a story? Write the event down the way it was told. Mull it over. See what other events are suggested—either from your life or your imagination. Write about that event, pretending you are writing to a reader who doesn't know you and will never meet you. (Hint: Even though you may feel psychically linked to the first-person narrator, it's helpful to remember that technically you are separate and this will help you work with the narrator's voice and give it range. The first-person narrator is the visible teller of the tale. You are the invisible shaper of the story. You must channel the story through the narrator's voice while finding ways to characterize the narrator.)

2. Remember something that happened to you when you were eight or younger. Write it down. Is it a one-liner with a moral twist? Or is there a sense of motion and transformation? If you think it's an anecdote, experiment with adding details, real or imagined, that will translate the event into a story.

3. Do the same exercise using lives of people you know, or fictional events.

4. Newspaper stories are often anecdotes. Read a story in the newspaper, and retell it as though it had happened to you. (Hint: Pretend that you're telling this story to someone who isn't familiar with the places being referred to, perhaps even someone who is from a different century. Try to describe people in vivid, concrete ways, instead of giving facts about them.)

As you do these exercises, you're starting to struggle with what *you* think a story is. Discovering the difference between an anecdote and a true narrative is an important breakthrough and gives you a profound understanding of what makes a story a story. Once you understand the difference between an anecdote and a story, you'll have a powerful tool for creating unity in all your fiction. And as you transform anecdotes into full-blown narratives you'll usually discover your themes, or the glue that binds the loosely linked events and answers the "So what?" behind every story.

Catalysts for the Story: Character-, Plot-, and Vision-Driven Stories

As you experimented with turning anecdotes into stories, you probably began to get a sense of what excited your interest. A family story about your great-grandfather wandering downtown in his bathrobe may not have turned into a story until you concentrated on the image of the bathrobe itself—noticed that it was sewn with an insignia of the French government and had pockets large enough to conceal weapons. Or the sense of the story may have begun when you heard a voice say: "Excuse me, sir, but can I direct you to the Salvation Army?" At this point your focus may have shifted to the other speaker—perhaps a retired schoolteacher who invites your great-grandfather home for tea—and you were launched into exploring a character. On the other hand, you may have remembered that your grandfather helped run a bookie operation, and his seemingly mindless journey may have turned into a complicated plot. Part of working with voice is learning what activates it—what arouses your imagination—and learning to trust your first instincts. The issue is always: What inspires you to tell a story? What is a point of departure for your voice?

When thinking about what energizes your voice, it's often useful to categorize novels and stories in the following ways: *character-driven, plot-driven,* and *vision-driven.* What catalyzes your voice is often what drives your story.

Ken Follett outlines his novels before he writes and doesn't even start to write until all the elements are in place. His sense of plot and structure is paramount, and his novels are masterful constructions of plot turns and surprises. Plot drives his stories and captivates his readers. Someone like Anne Tyler is a much more character-driven writer. In *The Accidental Tourist,* plot unfolds slowly. Her characters are what intrigue her, and because she sees them with such clarity, they intrigue us too. We're more tolerant of a slow-paced plot.

Plot-driven and character-driven stories are both fairly easy to characterize. Stories that are driven by other sources are harder to pin down. Terms like *image-driven, language-driven, idea-driven,* and *tone-driven* have all been used to talk about such stories. We've chosen *vision-driven* because it's the most inclusive.

Franz Kafka is a good example of a writer whose works are a complex weave of vision, ideas, tone, and imagery. His novel, *The Castle,* begins: "It was late in the evening when K. arrived. The Castle hill was hidden, veiled in mist and darkness, nor was there even a glimmer of light to show that a castle was there." K. cannot see the Castle and never arrives there. But this intriguing vision of "illusory emptiness" is a force through the entire novel. It's what the reader longs to see. It's what gives the main character, K., his sense of motivation. The castle is an inanimate object, yet emerges as a complex character, a fairy tale surrounded by red tape, the source of K.'s undoing. The plot unfolds as a truncated journey.

Stories that writers tell about how they write are a little like fishing stories, because part of the action occurs below the surface. So it's particularly audacious to guess what catalyzed another writer's story. Nonetheless, it's probably fair to say that some stories are shaped by ideas (like Italo Calvino's *Cosmicom-*

ics and *T-Zero*), others by a tone or point of view that pervades the entire piece without establishing definite, in-depth characters (many of Donald Barthelme's stories follow this pattern, including his novel *Snow White*). Others are driven by relationships where dialogue plays an important role: In Raymond Carver's short story "Whoever Was Using This Bed," a couple is awakened by a crank phone call in the middle of the night. They can't go back to sleep and get into a terrific wrangle about what to do if either of them gets sick and is put on life support. What emerges, through dialogue, is the frenzy of their relationship. Neither character is that clearly etched. But the relationship looms large, like a third person in the room, and the story is completely engrossing.

These categories are only frames and we encourage you to invent your own. It's important to emphasize that we're using them from a writer's perspective, not a reader's perspective. They're tools to help you think about your work, and they're not written in stone. For example, the voice of a character may incite you to start a story. Then, as a result of following something she says, you may develop a complicated plot, which is shaped by a poetic vision. Later, a reader may argue that you've written a vision-driven story, but you may have decided that the character became secondary as plot took over. Nonetheless, what catalyzes your voice is often what shapes your stories. And it's usually what gets you started. What we mean here by "getting started" doesn't necessarily refer to where a story begins. Sometimes the catalyst turns out to be the last scene and you have to write the story backward. Sometimes you have to write a story from the middle, working in both directions. The issue here is what generates potent material—not where that material ends up in your story.

Pay attention to whatever excites you, what propels you to daydream. For me, a story often begins with a character, such as a woman running down the street after the teenage daughter of a friend. I know this woman wants to talk to the girl, and the girl, who has curly red hair and is clutching an Indian basket handbag, is confused and wants to elude her. As I work I'll think about how these characters' actions propel a plot, but it's these initial characters that grab me and make me feel I have to write.

At other times a story starts because I've become fascinated by a single word like "camouflage." For a long time I think about the word and eventually see a series of images: a couple in Army camouflage fatigues; a government official in a suit that matches the colors of the Oval Office; a married woman in her thirties dressed like an upholstered chair in her living room. These images all suggest camouflage, but I don't know which to choose, if any, until some sentences appear: *She didn't remember exactly when she decided to make a dress that matched the colors of her favorite living room chair. Maybe one night when she was sitting in the living room reading. . . .* These sentences may be false leads, but they're enough to begin my story. The married woman moves forward. The government officials and the couple recede. Over a period of months, I've gone from a word to images to a single phrase. Ideas, language, and imagery have all determined the way I found my first character.

The key points of excitement that ignite your voice also influence the way you develop the story's other elements. In the story about the woman dressed like her chair, the way I develop characters and plot will be shaped by my fascination with camouflage. In the case where I'm drawn to the woman running after the teenage girl, the girl will become the main point of focus, at least initially. My challenge is to discover who she is and where she leads me. Plot and imagery will unfold as I discover what my character does and feels.

If you take a good look at the way you work, you'll probably notice that you work in many modes. If plot excites you, you may start with an outline, but at some point will need to translate this into scenes with concrete images and actions. You may even abandon plot for a while, as characters lead you in new directions. On the other hand, if your characters' dialogue or actions determine the beginning of your story, you may eventually need to impose more structure on your narrative than your character is providing. And if you're compelled by a phrase or image, you may need to work harder at developing characters and manipulating plot. Writers generally define the way they work by what makes them *want* to start a story, and this usually involves some aspect of voice that comes easily and feels spontaneous. There's a rightness to this: The first impulses to start a novel or story should feel compelling, enticing, urgent.

As you develop the voice that is uniquely your own, it's important to honor its first instincts. Notice what launches your voice, whether it's a luxuriant phrase, a plate of peaches, a complicated plot about a double agent, an idea about detachment and loneliness, or a character who talks about crocheting. These are important clues to the way your voice works and the kind of writer you are. Be receptive to writing different kinds of stories at different times. Don't feel compelled to write plot-driven thrillers like Stephen King or dense character studies like Thomas Mann just because you admire them. Write what you want to write. Do what you do naturally.

Working with Short Forms to Discover Your Story

You may have felt an instant sense of recognition when we described the difference between character-, plot-, and vision-driven stories: "Oh, yes. *Characters* are what spark my interest." Or: "It's *plot*. I love to imagine events pushing toward inevitable conclusions." Or: "All I ever start with is an *image*. I see a man who glows in the dark and I have to find out more." Or: "I have a specific sense of *tone*, a definite mood or feeling."

On the other hand, you may have wondered whether these distinctions could ever be useful to you. It's all very fine to talk about character-, plot-, and vision-driven stories. But if you don't know what *your* way of telling a story is, these categories may seem abstract.

Sometimes by experimenting with very short forms you're able to discover what kinds of stories you like to tell. These forms need be no more than a paragraph or two pages. Because they're so short, you often can finish them in a single sitting without letting the world of "real" time interrupt the fictional world you're trying to create. In this compressed atmosphere it's often easier to find out how your voice (particularly the part of it that functions as a composer) moves within a confined space. You see what propels voice forward, what gives your story its twist. You also get a chance to experiment with the rate at which you allow action to unfold, the rhythm of your language, and the way you handle transitions—those things that involve a story's pace and timing.

Here are some examples of short prose pieces that are shaped by very different elements. Reading them may help the categories we talked about earlier seem more concrete. You may also get a sense of how many ways there are for a writer's voice to tell a story:

1. In *The House on Mango Street,* Sandra Cisneros gets inside her main *character,* speaking from her voice and seeing the world through her eyes. The character shapes the story in short, complete single chapters. This chapter is called "Those Who Don't":

> *Those who don't know any better come into our neigh-borhood scared. They think we're dangerous. They think we will attack them with shiny knives. They are stupid people who are lost and got here by mistake.*
>
> *But we aren't afraid. We know the guy with the crooked eye is Davey the Baby's brother, and the tall one next to him in the straw brim, that's Rosa's Eddie V. and the big one that looks like a dumb grown man, he's Fat Boy, though he's not fat anymore nor a boy.*
>
> *All brown all around, we are safe. But watch us drive into a neighborhood of another color and our knees go shaikity-shake and our car windows get rolled up tight and our eyes look straight. Yeah. That's how it goes and goes.*

Notice how the character emerges. She is honest, a bit de-fiant. She notices a lot about other people, and uses names and specific details. Her sense of truth and a bit of futility shape the story. Her language is both tough and poetic.

2. Most *plot-driven* stories require length in order to develop fully. This is because plot-driven stories require carefully sketched events and a sustained sense of time. "The Eclipse" by Augusto Monterroso is notable because it's very short, yet driven by a dramatic situation that pushes the story to its conclusion. Here is the story in its entirety:

When Brother Bartolome realized he had lost his way, he knew that nothing could save him. The implacable Guatemalan jungle had trapped him for good. Faced with his ignorance of his surroundings, he sat quietly waiting for death. He would die there, hopeless and alone, with his mind firmly set on faraway Spain, and in particular on the convent in Los Abrojos, where King Carlos V had once condescended to step down from his eminence to express faith in his zealous missionary work.

When he awoke, he found himself surrounded by a group of impassive natives who were preparing to sacrifice him before an altar, an altar which Bartolome saw would be the final resting place for his fears, for his fate, and for himself.

Three years spent in the country had given him some command of the native languages, so he decided to try something. He spoke a few words, which the natives understood.

At that moment, an idea came to him that was truly worthy of his talent, his universal culture, and his profound knowledge of Aristotle. He remembered that a total eclipse of the sun had been predicted for that very day, and decided to use that secret knowledge to confound his oppressors and save his life.

"If you kill me," he told them, "I will cause the sun to darken in the sky."

The natives stared fixedly at him and Bartolome caught disbelief in their eyes. He waited confidently, not without contempt, as a small council gathered.

Two hours later, Brother Bartolome Arrazola's heart spilled its fiery blood onto the sacrificial stone (which glowed in the dim light of the eclipsed sun) while one of the natives, in a flat, unhurried voice, recited one by one the endless dates on which solar and lunar eclipses would occur, dates which the astronomers of the Mayan community had predicted and noted in their codices without any help from Aristotle.

(TRANSLATED FROM THE SPANISH
by William Rodarmor)

It's impossible to know how Monterroso wrote this story. However, the reader can see how a clearly defined situation—Bartolome's execution—defines the motion of the story and sets a series of events rolling in a logical sequence. Compare the urgency of voice in this tightly woven plot with a parody of plot in a prose-poem called "Incidents," by Danhil Kharms:

Once Orlov ate too many ground peas and died. Krylov found out about it and died too. Spirindov up and died all by himself. Spirindov's wife fell off the cupboard and also died. Spirindov's children drowned in the pond. Grandma Spirindov took to drink and hit the road. Mikhailov stopped combing his hair and caught a skin disease. Kruglove drew a picture of a lady with a whip in her hand and lost his mind. Perekhrestove was sent four hundred rubles by telegram and put on such airs that they fired him at his office.

Good people, but they don't know how to take themselves in hand.

(TRANSLATED FROM THE RUSSIAN
by George Gibian)

On the surface this looks like a tiny Russian novel in a paragraph. However it's the random, arbitrary order of events, rather than any kind of coherent sequence, that gives this prose piece unity. Again, we don't know how Kharms would describe writing this story. But the reader can see how the pace quickens and the images grow more bizarre as the story moves toward an increasing vision of chaos. This vision is underscored by the last line, *Good people, but they don't know how to take themselves in hand.*

3. Ana Hatherly, a Portuguese writer, uses *vision* and strong *imagery* to shape her prose pieces. Here are two examples from a remarkable series she wrote called *Tisanas*:

T I S A N A   # 8 2

Once upon a time there was a soft ladder. Everybody liked to go up it because it didn't tire them at all. When that model appeared on the market it was a howling success because everybody wanted to buy one to have in the house. Only much later the following generations understood the repulsive evil of the soft ladder. Then they conceived and executed the elastic ladder that not only didn't tire them at all but instantaneously returned them to the departure level. While on the soft ladder nobody managed to go down except by falling.

T I S A N A   # 8 7

Once upon a time there was a landscape where there were never any clouds. To make it rain it was necessary to wash the horizon with feathers.

(T R A N S L A T E D   F R O M   T H E   P O R T U G U E S E
b y   J e a n   R .   L o n g l a n d)

The imagery is outlandish, but the reasoning mimics the precision of a geometric proof. Hatherly allows the images to develop. She also takes surprising leaps.

4. David Ignatow, a poet and prose-poet, has written a short prose piece that is shaped by using a quirky point of view and a distinctive *tone*. This piece is called "I'm a Depressed Poem."

*You are reading me now and thanks. I know I feel a bit bet-
ter and if you will stay with me a little longer, perhaps take
me home with you and introduce me to your friends, I could
be delighted and change my tone. I lie in a dark drawer,
hardly ever getting out to see the light and be held. It makes
me feel so futile for having given birth to myself in antici-
pation. I miss a social life. I know I made myself for that. It
was the start of me. I'm grateful that you let me talk as much
as this. You probably understand, from experience; gone
through something like it yourself which may be why you
hold me this long. I've made you thoughtful and sad and
now there are two of us. I think it's fun.*

Notice how David Ignatow takes the point of view of an inanimate object. He addresses the reader directly from the confes-
sional quality he establishes at the beginning of the piece.

These examples illustrate how highlighting different elements
(plot, character, imagery) help shape a story and give it form.
To help you experiment, here are some ideas:

1. Write an autobiography in twelve sentences, using yourself, someone you know, or a fictional character. Now switch to
the third person and write a biography in twelve sentences.

2. Find an ad in the "Personals" section of a newspaper
that intrigues you. Write a one- or two-page story based on the
ad. Here are a few possibilities: 1) Write a letter that answers the
ad; 2) Write a journal entry from the point of view of the person
who wrote the ad; 3) Write a story about a first meeting between
the person who wrote the ad and someone who answers it.

3. Write an intimate scene in which two people are talking
about something significant to both of them, and let it consist entirely of dialogue. Make the time span of their conversation
short—about ten minutes. If it helps, make these people
intimately connected.

4. Write at least one of the following in no more than two pages: a mini-murder mystery, a mini-romance, a mini-historical novel, a mini-spy thriller, a mini-bodice ripper.

5. Write a chronicle of a fictitious family over a period of at least twenty-five years. Tell us about important events, possible scandals, secrets, deaths, weddings, and quarrels. Now write a similar chronicle of a royal dynasty spanning a period of one hundred years.

6. Write four fablelike stories told with as little dialogue as possible. Describe a journey into an imaginary terrain, a famous discovery, a war that changes a dynasty, or a miracle. Make the pacing brisk. (Hint: In working with image- or vision-driven stories, experiment with using the main image as a premise, and see what follows from it logically. Ana Hatherly's *Tisanas* are excellent examples of this technique.)

7. Write some confessions of inanimate objects: confessions of a pencil, confessions of a chair, confessions of Louis XIV's shoe. Write in the first person. Write quickly. Experiment with varying the mood and tone.

8. If you're a writer who becomes engrossed by longer forms, you can still learn about your voice by working with short forms. And here's another hint: Take two weeks off, go to a place where you'll be uninterrupted, and write a novel of at least one hundred and fifty pages very quickly. You'll make surprising discoveries about how your voice moves forward in a story.

Do these exercises in one sitting and try not to allow yourself to be interrupted. Don't stop when you're stuck. Don't put off the next scene until tomorrow. The point is to bring something to closure—not create a perfect work of art. This will help you discover what feels most natural and comfortable for your voice when it's working within a form. Which leads are most exciting to follow? Which paths bring your story to the most satisfying sense of completion? Notice what feels natural to your voice. Let it expand to create the shape of your story.

Point of View

Point of view is a primary vehicle for voice. Like voice itself, point of view is usually instinctive. I don't know why I speak in a first-person voice in one story, a third-person voice in another, or why in another I switch back and forth between multiple first-person voices. It's just the way the story comes out; the way I have to speak it at the moment.

Other writers I talk to say the same thing: Sometimes they may cast about to discover point of view, but usually it comes spontaneously, and there's a feeling that the story couldn't have been told any other way. In a sense, point of view—the vantage point from which you tell your story—*is* your story. To use a different perspective is to tell a different story.

For all its spontaneity, then, point of view has everything to do with intention. It's a choice that lets you tell the story *you want to tell*. It's a crucial aspect of the voice of the story: It will shape your story, determine its rhythms, tone, its impact on the reader, as well as what you can or can't present. If your story is told in the first person by chain-smoking fifty-year-old Selma who never leaves her apartment, you can't give a narrator's overview of the town she lives in or explore the inner life of her neighbor Ted, who brings her three cartons of Camels every time he goes to the grocery store and secretly wants to marry her. But if the story you want to tell is of Selma's cloistered life behind her velveteen drapes, Ted's inner thoughts aren't the point. A first-person point of view gives you the chance to create immediacy, to bring the reader into Selma's smoke-filled chambers, to feel the scratch of her nicotine-thickened voice, to be inside her rambling thoughts.

Try this: Take a story you've written in the first person and tell it with an omniscient narrator (or vice versa). How does the story change? Notice what the omniscient narrator can do that the first-person narrator can't. (He can move around more, see things a particular character couldn't see. He can comment on the story, give background information that would feel forced coming from a character.) Notice what the first-person narrator can do that the omniscient narrator can't. (She can create a stronger focus and greater sense of unity in the story. She can keep you closely connected to the inner experience of the character.) What point of view feels most natural for this particular story? Does the tone shift as you shift point of view? The language? The rhythms? Does the impact of the story change?

What you'll discover as you do this exercise is that *point of view is integrally connected to other elements of voice, such as narrative distance from the character, tone, vision, and rhythm.* Point of view may seem like a technical device, and to some extent it is. But when you settle on a "he" or an "I" or a particular character to tell your story, you're settling on much more than point of view. You're looking for the right blend of narrative distance, tone, pacing—all those things that voice is about.

Here's an example. Eudora Welty's famous story "Why I Live at the P.O." is narrated in the first person, by the daughter of a chaotic family in the rural South. "I just wanted to hear them talk," Welty says of her characters. And talk they do. The story begins:

I was getting along fine with Mama, Papa-Daddy and Uncle Rondo until my sister Stella-Rondo just separated from her husband and came back home again. Mr. Whitaker! Of course I went with Mr. Whitaker first, when he first appeared here in China Grove, taking "Pose Yourself" photos, and Stella-Rondo broke us up. Told him I was one-sided. Bigger on one side than the other, which is a deliberate, calculated falsehood: I'm the same. Stella-Rondo is exactly twelve months to the day younger than I am and for that reason she's spoiled.

The first-person narrator and her family argue and accuse, trade innuendos and threats. The spite and spittle of their dialogue *is* the story. If Welty had interrupted their spoon-waving tirades with a third-person narrator, she may have been able to give the reader an overview of the town or some insight into her character's history. But that wasn't what she wanted to do.

Welty's first-person dialogue also creates the rambling rhythms of her story, the humorous tone, and a narrative immediacy that makes the reader feel she's standing right in the kitchen with these characters, smelling the pickled tomatoes. This first-person voice, full of hyperbole and exaggeration, also builds the story's structure: a tall tale in which the characters' actions become increasingly melodramatic and absurd.

This is why point of view cannot be forced. It contains the crucial genetic material of the voice of the story. This is also why point of view can seem so central to a story, and why there's such a sense of relief when point of view feels right: because it means you've discovered other aspects of the voice of the story as well.

When I talk to students about point of view, I tell them to trust the point of view they instinctively began with. If a story begins in the mouth of sixteen-year-old Jason, let him take over. Usually there's a good reason why he was the one who started talking.

Yet every writer has had the experience at some time of feeling stuck with a story, of feeling that he/she is on the wrong track. Perhaps there's even a sense that the story simply won't be told the way you're going about it, as if you're trying to stick a square peg in a round hole. Gloria Naylor says when she was writing *Mama Day* she came to a place where she felt she couldn't write at all. She had written her first two novels, *The Women of Brewster Place* and *Bailey's Cafe,* in the third-person past tense, and she was determined to write her third novel that way, too. But she was stuck. One day, while trying to distract herself from her writer's block, she wandered into a public library and picked up a copy of Faulkner's *As I Lay Dying.* She suddenly realized the multiple viewpoint he used was what her story needed. It was a scary moment, because this shift meant she'd have to use a first-person viewpoint, which she hadn't done before, but she knew it was what she had to do.

Precisely because point of view is the key to so many crucial elements of voice, it can be a powerful point of experimentation. When you play with point of view, you're pushing yourself to discover what it is you really want to tell, and how. You're also learning how you work with voice differently, depending on how your story is told.

EXPERIMENTS IN POINT OF VIEW

Writers often use a first-person voice because it seems easier. You can write as if you're talking. The words are direct, and you avoid the technical issues of switching to a narrator. When you work initially with a first-person voice you may find that you can plunge more intimately into your material, stay closer to raw voice, and avoid the distanced tone of a narrator that often trips writers up. Try writing a story in the first person and see how it feels. Is voice easier or harder to access? Does the language feel more natural or forced? Are you enjoying yourself or does this voice feel awkward?

At other times you'll instinctively know that you have to write a story in the third person. You need to be able to drag the camera back and give a wide-angle shot. You need to be able to weave in and out of the thoughts of several characters. Or perhaps there's a feeling that you simply can't approach certain material in the first person. You need distance in order to engage the characters and their story. Or maybe the first-person voice always comes out sounding like you, the writer. You need a third-person voice to help you get out of yourself and into a character.

As you move your voice into the story, experiment with different viewpoints. In addition to switching between first and third person, try these improvisations:

1. Whether you're writing in the first or third person, switch your viewpoint to that of a different character. If a woman has been telling your love story, let the man tell it instead. Or tell it from the perspective of the woman's daughter, or of a cleaning person in whom one of the characters confides.

2. Tell your story from multiple perspectives. Give each person his or her own chapter or section. Have each character narrate a different part of the story, or have each one describe the same events, but from a different perspective.

3. Write a story or novel in which you alternate between first- and third-person sections. These sections may or may not be from the same person's point of view. Notice what parts you write in the first person and what parts you write in the third. How are these sections different? What made you want to make the shift? (Margaret Atwood wrote *The Edible Woman* in three sections, all from the point of view of Marian MacAlpine, the main character. The first and last sections are in the first person; the middle is in the third person. Atwood switches to third person in the middle of the book to reflect the way in which Marian has become disconnected from herself after agreeing to marry for the wrong reasons. Only when Marian breaks off the engagement does she say she can think of herself "in the first-person singular again." At this point in the narrative Atwood switches back to the first person.)

4. Write in the second person. Or write only some sections of your story in the second person. Notice which sections you changed to second person. Is there a pattern, something that links these particular sections, or that differentiates them from the sections you left as they were?

5. Create a character and then write about him or her from the point of view of an inanimate object (his watch, his Walkman, his jacket, his couch).

You'll discover that a different voice has different things to say, takes the story in a new direction, adds details, shifts tone. You'll feel the difference in your body, like running your fingers over a display of differently textured fabrics. You'll begin to get a feel for what a story demands of you, how you must use your voice to tell the story you want to tell.

CHAPTER TWENTY-SEVEN

Meeting the First-Person Narrator

Since the stories we first tell are usually about our lives, the first-person narrator is often the first storyteller we meet. This narrator's job seems easy. What could be simpler than telling a story about yourself?

This is often far from the case. Think back and consider what you needed to do when you worked with turning first-person anecdotes into stories: You had to create a character who could tell a story and be an embodied character in the story at the same time. If you used dialogue, your first-person narrator's voice had to function on at least two levels—the narrative "I," telling the story, and the dramatized "I," talking in the story. How did you work with these aspects of voice? Did the narrator's story turn out to be the same as the one you wanted to tell? Did you find it easy to embody a character modeled after yourself—someone whom the reader could see and hear?

E M B O D Y I N G   A N D
D R A M A T I Z I N G
T H E   F I R S T - P E R S O N   N A R R A T O R

First-person narratives, like journal entries, can trick you into writing in a kind of shorthand. It's easy to slip into the conventions we attach to the first person in colloquial speech, forget that you're separate from the narrator, and fail to create a character. This is particularly true if you model a first-person narrator after yourself. Because you know yourself, it's easy to assume that your readers will know the character. But readers can't supply a face, hear a voice, or know what someone looks like when they move around the room. The challenge is to make them believe in what happened and experience the first-person narrator as a full-blown, embodied character in the story he or she is telling.

One of my first stories was a first-person narrative modeled after my life. The story was about a woman who waits on tables while working on a thesis about Leibniz. Her boyfriend, an artist, drives a cab. When I gave the story to my friend, I confided to him that the main character "always returns to philosophy, because she finds the ordinary world cruel." This might have been a potentially interesting character. But instead of dramatizing her fascination with Leibniz, the story took place in a coffee house, where the narrator engaged in lengthy meditations on Leibniz—ranging from calculus to monads to divine and necessary truth. Interesting? Maybe to someone who's studied philosophers. But not to readers of fiction. Like a lot of first-person narrators, this narrator had very few characteristics. Her voice was suspiciously literary. After he read it, my friend said: "I wouldn't recognize this person in a crowd, even if she were wearing a red carnation."

Fortunately, my friend was a skillful teacher. He encouraged me to embody and dramatize the first-person narrator—and begin by observing myself. He suggested I take a good look at my apartment, notice the furniture, quality of light, experience myself as I moved through the rooms: What did I eat? When? How did I select my clothes? Did I put mail away as soon as I read it or did I let it gather dust on the kitchen table?

He also suggested that I engage in a little creative lying to get some distance from the narrator. "Why don't you have her live somewhere besides New York?" he said. "And let the boyfriend sell a little marijuana." Working with his suggestions was a stretch for my voice. I didn't want to release this narrator to the land of fictional characters. But eventually I created a character who surprised me, someone who said, directly to the reader: "If I weren't so shy, I'd invite you over for coffee." Someone who said to her boyfriend, while leafing through an underwear catalogue: "Leibniz sets the world to music. If he'd designed underwear, we'd all be dancing." Leibniz surprised me, too; instead of emerging as a dry abstract mind, he became a mirror for the character, echoing her desire for a hidden order. Lying had given me the courage to invent. It also brought me closer to the truth.

INCREASING THE RANGE OF THE FIRST-PERSON NARRATOR'S VOICE

When I rewrote this story, I made an interesting discovery about the first-person narrative voice in fiction: It has more range and freedom than the first-person voice in colloquial speech. In fiction you can twist, distort, embellish, and make things up—even when you have modeled a character after yourself. In colloquial speech, the moment you say "I," you're expected to tell the truth. In fiction, you're allowed to describe the obvious. If a first-person narrator tells a reader she has brown eyes and is wearing jeans, it may bring the character to life. When you're talking to someone and describe your appearance, it's redundant.

As my first-person narrator's voice developed more range, her priorities and urgencies as a storyteller became somewhat different from mine. Her style was less reverent. Her relationship with the reader was more intimate. At times, of course, I forgot that we were separate. At these moments our voices merged, resulting in prose that felt natural. But technically we *were* separate, and taking time to work with the distinction had increased the range of my voice and enriched my story.

Here are some things to try to increase the range of your voice when working with the first-person narrator:

1. For voice shifts: Create a fictitious first-person narrator and tell a story out loud in which you deliberately "throw" this narrator's voice like a ventriloquist to impersonate speech. Play with different possibilities, ranging from trying to duplicate your own speech to talking in a foreign accent. (Hint: It's often easiest to practice these voice-shifts when you work with a completely fictitious first-person narrator because it can be difficult to impersonate your own voice.)

2. For permission to lie: Tell a fictitious story in the first person, but pretend you're telling the truth. Remember that if you only dramatize what memory reveals, you may never write a story that has resonance for a stranger.

3. To practice embodying the narrator: Write a short paragraph describing something you do (playing basketball, cooking, reading). Use specific concrete details.

4. For narrative distance: Write some very short stories about your life before the age of fourteen. Try writing from your perspective now and your perspective then. Does one perspective give you more freedom to invent? Finding a voice with a comfortable temporal distance is often a key to writing a gripping autobiographical work in which you time-travel back to some point in your past and re-create the events, combining a more current perspective with an earlier perspective. This exercise can be helpful in finding that voice.

WORKING WITH A FICTITIOUS FIRST-PERSON NARRATOR

Some writers rarely use a first-person narrator modeled after themselves. In this case, it may be easier to create a first-person narrator who is a complete and satisfying character. But the writer's sense of the story's shape and ear for what feels urgent must still fuel the first-person narrator's voice.

Sometimes writers write a thin, sketchy, first-person story and insist "this is the way this character would tell a story in real life." It probably is. But it would bore a listener sitting on the town hall steps and it will also bore a reader. If you're working with a first-person narrator who is repressed, has little imagination, or is not a born storyteller, you have to do more work behind the scenes. You have to select vivid events for the narrator to mention, or get the narrator to be boring in ways that draw readers in. You're still channeling the story through the instrument of the first-person narrator's voice, but you're doing more work as the composer. You are making some independent choices about how the narrator's voice will select events; how his qualities will present themselves. This is an interesting tap dance, because you have to convince the reader that the narrator, not an invisible writer, is telling the story.

STAYING IN CHARACTER

No matter what kinds of narrators you work with, there will be times when your narrator's voice and point of view conflict with your own priorities as a writer. At these times it's tempting to push the first-person narrator aside, slip into his clothes, and use him as a vehicle for telling the story your own way. These moments may feel exhilarating, but they usually interrupt the story and pull the first-person narrator out of character.

It takes restraint and occasional cunning to keep a first-person narrator in character. Let's go back to Selma, the chain-smoking recluse mentioned in Chapter Twenty-six, "Point of View." Suppose Selma doesn't know her neighbor Ted buys her Camels because he wants to sleep with her? Suppose she thinks he buys Camels to collect coupons? In this case you have to work with Selma's voice to convey a situation she isn't aware of. For example, Selma may report a conversation in which Ted asks if she wants more Camels in a friendly, flirtatious way and Selma answers him stiffly. Or Ted may knock on her door, Selma may open it a crack, reach for the Camels, and shut the door abruptly. Selma's narrative style may be slow and somewhat dreamy. She may linger over details in her house—the way her cat looks lying in the sun, or dust on an embroidered pillow. But whenever Ted arrives the pace of her voice quickens. She becomes embarrassed, evasive.

To keep a first-person narrator in character it helps to have a clear sense of their voice. A narrator who says: *The silk of my mamma's dress makes me feel like I'm swimming in a river* would probably never say *The extraordinary thing about duality is that it's an omnipresent ghost.* Try not to interrupt the first-person narrator with your own literary flights. If you strongly disagree with the way a first-person narrator is telling a story, create a character whose voice is more in harmony with the natural impulses of your own voice.

A first-person narrative voice may be easier to create if you speak it out loud. Deliver monologues. Create scenes with friends. Consider taking a class in improvisation.

VOICE AND NARRATIVE RELIABILITY

In many cases a fictional first-person narrator is a reliable story-teller. When the character in *Moby Dick* starts the novel with the line "Call me Ishmael," you know you've met a narrator who'll tell you a great metaphysical tale from the point of view of an ordinary seaman. Alice Munro's character, Rose, in *The Beggar Maid* is a more sophisticated narrator, with thorny parts to her personality. Yet she's able to see her own foibles, self-deceptions, even cruelties, with a pitiless eye. In this case readers delight in Rose's searing self-honesty.

In other stories the first-person narrator may tell us things that don't quite tally with his or her actions in the story, or possibly with the story itself. Sometimes this discrepancy is the result of deliberate concealment, as when the narrator in Par Lagerkvist's extraordinary novel, *The Dwarf,* deliberately doesn't reveal his treacherous plans, even though he knows them. Sometimes it's the result of naiveté or self-delusion. In Kazuo Ishiguro's novel, *The Remains of the Day,* the first-person narrator, Stevens, sincerely believes he's telling you a true story, but is supremely self-deluded.

According to his own lights Stevens is an impeccable butler in a stately mansion. But the more he describes his life the more we see he lives without compassion or morals. After his father dies, Stevens carries on with his duties, not pausing for an instant; when his master entertains high officials, Stevens feels privileged to serve them—even though a few are Nazis. As the story continues, Ishiguro, the writer behind the scenes, emerges as a more deeply felt presence. This is accomplished through skillful voice shifts, careful scene building, and the way Ishiguro shapes Stevens's depiction of himself. Ishiguro remains unseen, like an impeccable butler at his own dinner party. Yet his subtle shaping of the story allows the reader to experience him as a moral ally and enjoy him as a secret companion. Ishiguro's vision is ironic and undeceived, quite different from the vision of Stevens. Nonetheless, Stevens's extreme desire to be an exemplary butler gives him a convincing motive as a narrator: He wants the reader to see him just the way he sees himself. Ishiguro exploits this trait and never fails to convince us that Stevens is telling the story.

Dickens also uses the deluded first-person narrator in many

of his novels. In *Great Expectations,* events that seem trivial to Pip are etched so clearly, the reader sees Pip's delusions long before Pip does.

Using an unreliable narrator may give your voice an even wider range in a first-person story. Through small inconsistencies between what the narrator says he does and how he shows himself in action, as well as through skillful voice shifts and changes in pacing, the writer's perspective becomes a pervasive, if inaudible, presence. This is an instance in which the writer's voice may function more actively as the composer of an entire story, even though it is working through the voice of a character.

To further increase the range of the first-person narrator's voice, create a character who is strikingly different from you and put him or her in a simple scene (for example, in a bedroom with a lover, or on a bus with a stranger). Allow some disagreement to ensue and have the character tell a story about it. Experiment with a first-person narrator who tells us a believable story and a narrator who omits, conceals, or shows a strongly flavored bias. Be sure to experiment with characters who deliberately lie as well as those who are naive or self-deluded. Notice how you, the writer, find ways to shape your story.

As you work with dramatizing the first-person narrator, you'll begin to create vivid characters. These are narrators you'll always recognize in crowds—with or without carnations.

Working with Third Person: Discovering a Narrative Persona

Working with a third-person narrator can be one of the trickiest parts of working with voice in the story. "I can hear my characters," writers often say, "but I just can't hear how this narrator should talk. The narrator's voice feels wooden."

Unlike the voice of characters, this narrator's voice isn't embodied. It's a voice that pipes up from the sidelines to move the story along, offer description, provide wry comments or pertinent information, set a tone, and enlist the reader's interest. But who does this voice belong to? It's not the author, and it's not the characters. Giving this narrator a persona of its own—indeed, recognizing that it even has a persona—is one of the challenges of working with a third-person voice.

Here's the opening paragraph of a young adult novel written in the third person:

> *The envelope lay unopened on her dresser. Willie Murray glared at it from time to time as if the force of her gaze would make it disappear. While she packed racquets, tee shirts, warm-up pants and tennis skirts in a large red*

*duffel bag, Willie directed angry thoughts at the letter. I
don't need you. . . . As if I didn't have enough on my mind.
. . . Why'd you have to arrive now? She dropped down,
looking under her bed for her tennis shoes. They weren't
there, but something else was just behind the dust ruffle.*

The narrator's voice is doing a lot in this first paragraph:
introducing the main character, describing her actions, sketch-
ing details of the scene, creating tension, and evoking the character's inner feelings. Notice how close to Willie the voice is. It's
right there with her looking under the bed. It's inside her mind
feeling her tension. Notice how the narrator speaks almost as
Willie would, in the unpretentious language of a teenager.

When the narrative voice is right in the scene, closely linked
to the character it's describing, it most readily takes on the persona of the character whose shoulder it looks over. The prose
feels seamless. The reader is almost unaware that a third presence is there. And the writer, having a character as a guide, more
easily accesses and grounds this third-person voice.

But the narrator's voice can't always be close to a character.
There are times when you want the narrator's voice to have a
different perspective from that of your characters, in order to
create irony, tension, or humor, such as when the narrator interrupts a dinner-party scene to comment on a noodle, hanging
like seaweed from the chin of the elegantly dressed hostess. At
other times, you may want your narrator to step out of the immediate scene and provide a wide-angle view that a character
couldn't see. If you're evoking a landscape, for instance, your
narrator needs to be able to swoop back and away to describe
the stretch of horizon.

Notice the difference in narrative distance (the distance between the narrator and the characters) in these passages:

1. It was the winter of 1993. A solitary figure walked
through the snowy streets of Manhattan.

2. Edward Tolliver leaned into the wind. The cold sliced though his coat as he walked through the snow to Tracy Covey's house on Jane Street.

3. A sick heat spread through Edward's chest, though the snow whipped in sharp slices across his face and coat. His fingers touched the letters in his pocket. He didn't want to show them to his cousin. Everything he'd hoped to hide was there.

In the first example, the narrator seems to be floating high above the roofline, gazing down on the snowy streets. In the second, the narrator strides alongside Edward. By the third, the narrator's voice inhabits Edward's body, experiencing the sick heat in his chest and fingering the letters in his pocket. The voice seems to be that of Edward himself. But who does the voice in the first example belong to? What tone should it have? What attitude should it have toward the story it's telling?

Finding the right narrative voice can be most troublesome when the narrator has a great deal of distance from the characters being described. The distanced voice tends to float free, not be grounded, and it easily becomes a voice of the head—an imposter voice. The voice of the narrator starts to explain, justify, give information in a dry, cerebral way. It says, "Evan often felt that his mother was the cause of his anxiety" (distanced from the body, a "head" voice), instead of "Evan felt a brush of brassy light, as if his mother's willow switch still swung for his bare legs" (close to the character, sensory, rhythmic).

D I S C O V E R I N G   A
N A R R A T I V E   P E R S O N A

As with any aspect of voice, discovering the voice of your narrator is always connected to finding something in yourself. The narrator is a persona developed from deep spontaneous elements within the writer: quirks, world view, sense of language, balance between thought and emotion. It's another way the writer projects himself into the story, giving voice through this third presence to parts of himself that couldn't surface through the characters.

Take a story you've written with a third-person narrator and read it aloud, listening for the places where the narrator steps in to add comments, give background information, or move the story forward. Notice the tone of your narrator's voice. Is it dry and cerebral, or does it pulse with the rhythms of the story? Does it have your distinctive cadence, your sense of rhythm and language? Does it have a personality? Does it breathe?

Imagine this narrator as a character. What would this character wear? Bright or somber colors? How would he sit or stand? What tone of voice does he project? Does she have a sense of humor? Is he a cynic or a sentimentalist? Emotional or restrained? Would she get up early or late? Does she smoke and swear? Does he go to church?

If you can't imagine your narrator as a character, his voice may be too generic. Give your narrator a personality. Let him introduce himself, tell you what he had for breakfast. Rewrite the passage with this character in mind.

No matter what kind of narrator you have, you want this voice to have the same energetic presence as any other voice in your story. It must be connected to the blood-rhythms of the body. It must have cadence, carry emotion. Write a monologue in the voice of your narrative persona, letting him divulge his feelings about the story he's telling.

I have a narrator's voice inside me that's always ready to pipe up with the beginning of a story (though getting him to finish one is a trial). Here's something he spoke spontaneously:

One night after placing his slippers side by side and sliding into bed with his wife, Frederick decided to tell her of his worst fear. He switched on the light and watched the bundle of covers next to him sag with his wife's slow breathing. He was not sure what had brought him to this moment of unburdening, he only knew that suddenly the

telling seemed preferable to the not telling. He shook her
gently.

I imagine this narrator as a slightly balding man who wears a tweed vest and sits in an overstuffed chair with his legs crossed. Despite his formality, he has a wry sense of humor and insight into his characters. His tone is matter-of-fact, a bit detached, which seems right for presenting my poor Frederick.

Later, though, as I thought about this nattily dressed narrator, I became aware of the oratorical quality of his voice. In this story, which felt like a parable, that tone seemed right. In other ones, I might want to shake up this narrator, push him to be more contemporary and colloquial.

I never thought of this narrator as a character while I was writing. He simply spoke, and I recorded. But personifying him as I look back on the story helps me ground this voice in a body (and feel where it resides in *my* body—in my chest, in this case). It helps me listen to the narrator's speaking rhythms, to his tone, and to feel the way he uses language. Then if I want to tweak some part of his personality, I can. I can dress him in a T-shirt and jeans, make him younger. Or I can send him back to central casting altogether.

Here are some other questions you might want to ask yourself as you write in the third person:

1. What kind of narrative distance do I want? Is my story told best by a narrative persona that can see things the characters can't, can have attitudes the characters don't have—to create irony, tension, humor, or compassion? Or is the story told best by a narrator who is very close to one or more of the characters? If so, have I kept the narrator's persona close to that of the character, using the language the character would use, thinking the thoughts as my character would think them? (Often, of course, you'll shift narrative distance within a story.)

2. Is my narrator's voice grounded in sensory detail? Does it emerge from my body and breath, not my head?

3. Does it have a sense of rhythm? Can I read it aloud and feel its musicality, its sense of phrasing?

4. Does it convey a particular tone? Does this tone shift when the emotional energy of the story shifts?

5. Have I used the narrator's voice more than I need to? Does it too often interrupt the action of the story? If so, are there places where I can omit it? For instance, if the narrator is frequently used to give background information, can I present this information through the character's dialogue or thoughts? Or can I omit the information altogether?

6. How does this narrative persona feel about the story he/she's telling? Would she want to have the main character over for dinner? What would they talk about if she did?

The tone of your narrator's voice, its rhythms, its attitude toward the story it's telling (whether it views the characters with compassion or disgust, humor or anger), the narrative distance—these are all qualities of the narrator that you discover as you're telling your story. As with characters, a whole host of narrative personae live inside of you, and each one is going to tell a story differently. Get to know these personae. Take them out to lunch. See what they have to offer.

Secrets as a Key to Character

> His *mind of man, a secret makes*
> I *meet him with a start*
> He *carries a circumference*
> In *which I have no part*
>
> — E M I L Y D I C K I N S O N

A fully alive character is never completely revealed, but is like an interior of a house glimpsed only through windows. A compelling part remains unseen—open to mystery, intrigue, and speculation. Characters think to themselves, dream, have memories; they have an autonomous life that you, the writer, are not a part of. In crucial ways, they live beyond you.

When you work with characters in a story, whether you're writing in first or third person, your voice needs to be loose, open to your characters' improvisations, so that this vital inner world can be spontaneously revealed. You may at times manipulate your characters for effect within a story (you know that at the end of the scene you're writing Juno will run into Sam, whom she's desperately trying to avoid, because you need a dramatic clash), but at the same time, you give your characters autonomy. You remain open to what your voice brings forth, unplanned. (Sam slaps a dollar bill on the coffee table. He's nervous. You don't know why.)

This receptiveness to a spontaneous voice within yourself has a lot to do with your ability to project yourself fully into your character, and to leave yourself behind. It has to do with living in your character's body and listening for his inner voice—the one that emerges in strange and secretive ways.

REVEALING SECRETS

One of the best ways to discover what characters speak only to themselves is to ask them to tell you their secrets. They may not tell you all their secrets. But if you listen, you'll begin to get a sense of their private interior world—a world that's partially hidden. As they talk—or even refuse to talk—they'll be revealing themselves on their own terms. You'll also get practice in the art of putting yourself aside and projecting your imagination onto another person. The secrets they offer will be their own, not yours.

Take a character whose voice you've heard speaking inside you, whom you want to get to know. If she's willing, give her a name and put her in a specific place, a specific time, and specific circumstance. However, if she seems uncomfortable and the details or name feels forced, let her remain vague. (Characters can evolve differently.) Now ask yourself a few initial questions: What is she wearing? How is she feeling at this very moment? What happened just before this moment? How do you feel in her presence?

When you (and she) feel ready, start the interview. Here are some questions you might ask:

1. What are some mistaken impressions people have about you?
2. What are some correct impressions?
3. What secret about yourself do you most want to keep?
4. What secret about someone else is the most distressing for you to keep?
5. Tell me about a time you did something you now wish you could have done differently.

6. What frightened you most when you were small?
7. What frightens you most now?
8. Do you have a secret ambition?
9. Do you have a secret you've never revealed to anyone?

Listen to your character with interest and detachment. Watch her for a while, as she moves about her life. What do you trust about her? What do you mistrust? Does she ever lie? What isn't she telling you? Often the apparent, surface words or details mask something deeper and more complex.

William Styron says that halfway through the writing of *Sophie's Choice* he realized that his main character, Sophie, was lying to her new friend Stingo about her family and her past. She had fabricated the wonderful stories she'd told Stingo of her happy childhood in Poland and how her father was a hero to her because he'd tried to save the Jews. In fact, her father was a rabid anti-Semite. This realization, for Styron, was a turning point. He suddenly glimpsed Sophie's vulnerable, injured inner self and knew her need to create the picture of a noble father hid a deeper truth. At this moment he had to be willing to let his character become someone different than he thought her to be. Slowly, as Styron wrote, Sophie began revealing other secrets about her past, culminating in the shocking end to her story. Because Styron trusted her, his story became more explosive.

This summer I did an improvisation exercise with a group of writers in which four of them agreed to create themselves as characters and the rest agreed to be interviewers. These four were instructed to create characters with secrets they didn't want to reveal. The rules were loose: The characters could know the secrets or be in some form of denial about them. The secrets could range from passions, obsessions, visions, crimes, to aspects of family life.

At the end of the complete interview series, each character delivered a monologue, revealing his or her secret. I was struck by the way the secrets influenced responses to the questions—even when the questions weren't directly related to what was being concealed. For instance, one writer created a teenage character who had seen an angel walking up Telegraph Avenue. The teenager believed that the angel was real, but was embarrassed by his belief. He masked this with evasive answers to all kinds of unrelated questions as well as a posture of cynicism. Another character was a ninety-year-old woman in a convalescent home who told outrageous stories about stolen jewelry to mask, from herself as well as the group, the fact that her son had stopped coming to visit her. It became clear that secrets link up with hidden biases and agendas, and often have a pervasive influence on the way characters act and reveal themselves.

C O N C E A L I N G   S E C R E T S

Even as you probe your characters, and project yourself into their inner worlds, you want to let them keep an aura of mystery. Your acquaintance with these characters, as writer or reader, should be like an exciting love relationship: There's enough intimacy to keep you satisfied, enough mystery to keep you coming back for more.

As you let characters loose and listen to them tell their stories, you can capitalize on the double-edged power of secrets: discovered secrets propel action and lend excitement; withheld secrets create an urgent desire to learn more. You get to know your characters deeply, intimately, and you allow them to elude you. You live with them, eat with them, sleep with them, and let them have a secret life of their own. If you find it useful to write biographical sketches of your characters, do so. But allow your characters to grow beyond your initial impressions. Keep an eye out for the unexpected things your characters do or say— these are potential hints about your story. Use these hints to propel a new scene or plot development.

1. Write a story which begins just as a character reveals a secret, and continues because this character keeps another secret hidden. Don't worry about what this second secret is as you write. Let yourself be surprised.

2. Create two characters: one who confesses everything about himself, another who confesses nothing. Put them in a car together as they're driving to a family reunion.

3. Create a character who tells a secret to one person, but hides it from another. Let these two people—the one who knows the secret, and the one who doesn't—have coffee together and talk about the person who told the secret to one of them.

4. Arm a character with a vital secret—unknown to you, the writer—and send him into a small town or city that you know well. Abandon him there, and see what he discovers.

For the reader as well as the writer, tension comes from this process of continuing discovery. You want to tell enough to interest the reader, hold back enough to entice. Learn to reveal important clues about your characters at just the right moment—when they will heighten suspense, affect another character, advance the plot, or push the conflict in a new direction—not too soon. And never tell your reader more (about the character, the character's background, the history of the times) than he absolutely must know at any given moment in order to follow the story. The desire to dump into the story everything you, the writer, know about your characters and their history (you spent five months in France researching war memoirs, and you're damned well going to include everything you learned if it kills you!) will end up killing the story. Let the aura of secrets guide your voice.

Finding Dialogue through Impersonation

Just as your character's inner voice is richly revealing, so is your character's outer voice—his dialogue—laden with double-meaning, nuance, and implication. When you home in on what is important in dialogue you hear not only what is being said (and not said), but how it's being said. You're aware of interruptions, how people don't listen. You hear someone being indirect, or challenging, or taking center stage. You notice how people talk past each other. "Mother, I quit my job." "Do you want more stew, darling?"

Everyone has distinctive conversational mannerisms or strategies. (She says: "Do you think it's cold in here?" when she wants the window closed. He says, "Close that damned window!") And everyone has a subtext to what they say. ("Close that damned window!" could mean "I expect to have things my way," or it could mean "I'm mad at you for not having sex with me.") By capturing these distinctive markings as you write dialogue, you reveal something about your character as well as something about the emotional drama of the moment.

Great impersonators throw aside their own way of talking and take on the voice of another. As you work with character, letting yourself become possessed by this person, you want to abandon the automatic voice in your head that offers dialogue as *you* would speak it, and become the voice of this other person. Begin by quieting your own speech and absorbing what you hear around you. Spend a whole day listening to someone of the opposite gender, of another generation, or another ethnicity. Notice the difference between the way you talk and the way they do. What is something they would never say? How often do they ask questions? Do they express feelings directly? Do they speak briefly or are they long-winded? Are they hesitant or direct? Do they use particular "sayings" or colloquialisms? How is their cadence distinctive? Listen for what is not said as well as what is said; listen for the meaning of silence.

As you listen, notice how the body participates in speech. High-strung Mrs. Kinnard always talks a mile a minute, finishes your sentences for you, and waves her hands. Arnie Slater swallows his words and never looks at you. Your voice is influenced by your relationship to your body. So are the voices of your characters. The more deeply you're grounded in a character's body, the more easily you'll capture his distinctive speech.

Ill Will as a Source of Monologue

It's often easiest to hear a person's conversational trademarks when you're listening to someone who irritates you. The voice of someone who drives you crazy scratches around in your head like an irksome grain of sand and invades your very being. You remember every nuance, every annoying twang, every discordant clearing of the throat. I can call to mind in an instant a teacher from high school whose high-pitched nasal whine ("That's easy for you to say, you don't have to support yourself") came incongruously from a pale, lovely face while she swung her nylo-ned leg. Usually characters like this stick with you for a reason: They're highly flavored, powerful personalities. They're wonderful candidates for imitation.

Evoke the voice of a character you don't like, whose words set you on edge. Speak a monologue out loud in the voice of this character. Allow your body to get into the act. Feel the person's facial tic. Use her hand gestures. Become this person. Let yourself be possessed. Sometimes just allowing yourself to imagine you are possessed is a trigger for monologue, but if you can't think of anything to say, try a lecture or diatribe. ("Clean your room!" "People these days aren't willing to work!") Or let this person discourse on an imminent visit from a relative she despises.

The people you knew in childhood—usually grown-ups—offer great possibilities for this exercise. Children aren't nearly as good at shutting people out as adults are, and their experience of other people—and the voices of other people—is much more visceral. Remember a despised neighbor, or your mother when she found out you'd raided her make-up kit on Halloween. Throw yourself into her body, and get her to talk, speak out loud. Now try a written monologue.

By now you'll have discovered that animosity is a greatly underutilized power source. Once you're revved up, keep going. Introduce a second character and write a dialogue, seething with hostility, in which the two discuss the weather and the price of strawberries. Make their anger indirect, but powerfully appar-ent. Now have them argue about something openly, such as how to cook a ham.

Dialogue is a dance, a choreographing of a relationship. As you write dialogue, you want to feel what it's like to be in a character's body, responding to someone else. Sense the way the character is being heard, and how that will influence his next response. Notice how he answers back.

Here are some more improvisations to help you slip into the body and voice of another person:

1. Write a monologue in the voice of a friend or acquaintance of yours who is a recent arrival in this country, in which he expounds on what American habit upsets him the most. Capture his speaking rhythms, mannerisms, and inflections.

2. Think of someone you know who always tries to tell you what to do. (You say you have a sore throat, she immediately tells you about the remedy she uses that you too must take.) Now think of someone you know who is more easygoing. Write a conversation between the two of them as they assist a woman in labor.

3. Have a man at a party tell jokes after having been rejected by a woman he's attracted to. Feel how the rejection stings. Capture his forced enthusiasm, or his awkwardness, or his smoothness. Then rewrite the scene, so the character tells jokes after having been encouraged by the woman he's attracted to. Notice how he relaxes, or becomes buoyant, or nervous.

LETTING GO OF YOUR PROGENY

It's easy to feel possessive of the characters you create, to feel that they're yours and should serve your purposes. When you stand outside your characters, as the writer thinking about your story, you may tend to manipulate characters. You let them talk about the meaning of your story, or explain your theme. You use them as instruments rather than letting them have a life of their own. You, the author, may want to write about the competition and strain between two sisters, but left to their own devices, your characters will argue over a Christmas gift. You may want to explore the tensions surrounding the break-up of a marriage, but the unhappy couple talks about redecorating the nursery.

Resist the temptation to speak for these characters—to put dialogue in their mouths that is really what you, the writer, are thinking about or want to say about your story. Learn to spot the character who talks endlessly about the plot, or expounds upon the writer's ideas—he's a front man for the author. Characters need to be oblivious to the ultimate meaning of their story. Let them simply go skeet shooting, swat a fly, or yell at Danny for leaving the door open.

Surrendering to your characters takes a leap of faith: You must believe that their thoughts, words, and actions will convey the story adequately, so the reader "gets it." But it's precisely this surrender that gives them a chance to become themselves. At the same time that you find your voice, you relinquish voice to your characters.

Voice and Tone

With the mail and manuscripts at my office this week arrived two long-awaited packages. I edged a knife along the snug corregated cardboard and fished out from each a crisp book—first novels by clients of mine. That delicious sawdusty odor of new books rose from the pages as I flipped through them. How satisfying to run my fingers over the waxy cover, the familiar words in such clear ink. I'm always amazed at how authoritative words seem when typeset. I swept aside a clutter of papers on my desk and sat down. Even though I'd read these novels over and over in manuscript form, I was struck by the strength of voice in each of them, and by the unique tone each projected, right from the beginning.

> He came to the beach that day. I didn't really think he would. He had sort of agreed to meet me there, but I didn't give him very good directions. As I was carrying my chair and straw bag over to the sand dunes where the empty sailboat sat high on the beach by the houses, I

*realized that it wasn't 26th Street—it was 23rd Street. I
was three whole streets off.*

I thought, he's absolutely never going to find me.

—SOFIA SHAFQUAT, *THE SHADOW MAN*

*I had already lost her when the anxiety attacks began. I
said, "I am hyperventilating again, Cecilia."*

*"Breathe, and feel your feet resting solidly on the
floor," she says.*

*I throw myself at her feet and move slowly up her
legs. My head is almost on her inner thigh when she begins
to pull my face up her stomach, all the while smoothing
the sweat from my burning forehead. I notice the delicate
square fingers and the turquoise ring lighting up her left
hand. And I see that her lifeline is longer than mine.*

—MADELINE MOORE, *AS YOU DESIRE*

Sophia: colloquial, casual. She uses phrases like "sort of" and
"three whole streets off." Madeline: intense, erotic. The language is poetic: "turquoise ring lighting up her left hand." The
narrator is swept by impassioned feelings. In each, the tone gives
me an instant feel for the writer's sensibility, and prepares me
for the kind of story that's ahead.

Tone is one of the most distinctive elements of your voice,
having intimately to do with who you are as a writer, and what
kind of story you're writing. A light fanciful idea is written with
a light tone. A serious subject is rendered with a darker, more
intense tone. Certain styles have more depth of tone. Others
have a breezier touch. Like a drop of ink in a glass of water,
tone gives your writing coloration. If you know a writer well,
you'll recognize the voice by its tonal qualities just as you recognize a familiar voice over the telephone, or your favorite
singer. In fact, as a reader you often choose favorite authors
because you're drawn to their tone.

As you write your stories, you'll be discovering your voice's
tonal qualities and learning how to work with them. You don't

force a tone that isn't you. You honor your voice's natural ca-
pabilities. You don't try to write with the sophisticated intellectual absurdity of John Barth if your voice more naturally speaks
like a colloquial, earthy Bobbie Ann Mason. At the same time,
you're always working to develop your voice's tonal range, to
discover the hidden corners and capacities of your voice that at
first may not be apparent.

A singing student may feel uncomfortable straining for high
notes. She'll complain that it hurts to reach that high. Her muscles tense and ache. When she's able to relax and realize that
her voice wants to go up there, her muscles work naturally.
Those high notes become a part of her range.

S T R E T C H I N G   Y O U R   R A N G E

Read over a number of your stories. Become aware of what tone
or tones you adopt most easily. Write a list of words which characterize these tones. Distanced and bitter. Jaunty but jaded. Gay.
Serious and thoughtful. Sarcastic. Disaffected and nihilistic. Any
adjective that describes the feel of your writing is an aspect of
tone.

The tones that permeate your writing may be the true marks
of who you are as a writer, the result of letting your voice work
naturally. But your natural voice, the one that comes easily, may
not be your fullest voice. As you're learning what your voice can
do and how it works best, you may find, like the singer unsure
of high notes, that there are more notes you can hit.

After you've noticed the tones you most easily adopt, notice
what you avoid. Do you seldom write in a flat, journalistic tone?
Or a comic tone? Or a tragic tone? Try it! Write a short sketch
in a tone that is different from your other stories. Or rewrite a
story in an opposite tone. If it was humorous and light make it
more pointed and probing. If it was restrained, make it more
exuberant.

A student once rewrote a story that had been quite abstract

and lyric, using a more colloquial, humorous tone. Instead of phrases like "bright, shimmering radiance," she used words like "root-beer," and "all this stuff." A character who had reclined pensively under a tree now collected cans in a junkyard. When she read it to the class, sitting nervously on the edge of her seat, she had us in stitches. She was astonished. "I didn't know this story could be funny." Then she added, "I didn't know *I* could be funny." By shifting tone you often discover, as this woman did, that you open up hidden corners of your personality, and bring them into your work.

Here's another exercise: Read a story you've written and ask yourself what kind of person would tell the story in this particular way. What persona do you imagine behind your story? A somber-faced journalist? A hip young woman in high-heeled boots? Adopt a different persona and tell the story again. You'll quickly notice that different personae evoke different tones.

I began to understand the connection between persona and tone when, in 1979, I clomped into the tiny basement office at San Francisco State where I was to be grilled for my master's orals, decked out in leather boots and tight jeans. "You're so different from your writing!" one of my professors said as I settled jauntily into a hardback chair stuffed between cartons of unsold student magazines and shelves crammed with Shakespeare and Dante.

I was startled by his comment, and didn't know quite what to make of it. After a while what he meant dawned on me. He knew me as someone who leapt into discussions, was gregarious and challenging. Once I'd almost come to blows with a classmate when he used a woman's poem as a chance to deliver an astounding tirade on vaginal odors. The stories and poems I was writing, though, were quiet and lyric, the tone somber. Both personae (the animated student and the brooding poet) were me. But only one—my more private, darker persona—was creating the tone of my writing.

Once I realized this I began to experiment. I played with persona and worked to bring more range into my work. Sometimes I still give over to my darker inner self. It feels honest. Other times I push myself to draw on both my public and private personae, to tap all parts of myself as I write.

For each writer the struggle to access and define a tonal range is different. Sometimes you have to throw out myths and ideas—perpetuated by your family, your upbringing, your community—about what kind of person you're supposed to be and what kind of writer you're supposed to be. Sometimes you have to work against your own self-censorship. Many writers purposefully efface parts of their personality that they don't like, or imagine are unattractive, by adopting a tone that masks these parts. You use a light-hearted tone to hide your bleak feelings, a hip tone to mask your insecurity. Working with tone can be a liberating way to bring a fuller, more powerful presence into your work.

When you fool around with tone, you'll discover, too, that characters may change, new characters emerge, or the plot takes a new direction. Tone affects what you focus on in a story—what details you leave in or out—as well as how you present those details. When you write a scene in a humorous tone about a couple's fight over what to save as their house burns, he'll dash inside to grab his collection of antlers. When you write it more seriously, she'll try to save the family photos. So experimenting with tone is also a way to mine for content—to discover something about a character or plot you hadn't known before.

TONE AND NUANCE

Once you develop a consistency, you work to build on that, to put emotion and nuance on top of your basic tone. The tone of a murder mystery may be boisterous and wise-cracking as it begins, but when the emotional high points unfold, the tone becomes more serious. A deeper side of a character is revealed. This ability to manipulate tone for emotional effect within a story is one of the hallmarks of a strong narrative voice. It develops over time, like voice itself, as you come to know how to align your tonal emphasis with the emotional moment within your story.

Interestingly, this is one of the places where a writer's strength of tone can get in the way. A writer who is riotously funny may not be as good at evoking a more heartfelt tone when the story calls for it. A writer who is great at poetic riffs may need to punctuate them with a more colloquial tone to keep from being too precious. If you instinctively have a powerful and consistent tone you may need to push yourself to discover the range of emotion you're capable of.

Try this: Listen to a piece of your favorite music, whether it's rock, opera, jazz, or classical. Close your eyes and feel the emotional movement of the piece in your body. What emotion do you feel as the piece begins? As it builds? Where are the crescendos? The relaxations? Feel how the musical tones—the shadings and rhythms—reflect this movement.

Read a story by one of your favorite authors. Notice the places within the story where the tone shifts (when the plot shifts; when a character makes a revelation about himself or someone else; when the action speeds or slows; when a new character or situation is introduced). When the tone shifts, how does the language change? The prose rhythms? The details of scene?

Go back to a story or chapter of a novel you've written and notice where an emotional turning point occurs. (Usually this coincides with a turning point in the action—for example, a man has his head under the hood of his Toyota pickup when he hears a squeal coming from the barn. He leaps up. The pace quickens. The tone becomes more urgent.) Does the tone shift to emphasize this turning point? Does an ironic tone become shaded with deeper feeling? Is a light tone colored with greater excitement?

Remember: Tone doesn't necessarily *parallel* content. A violent story may be told in a matter-of-fact tone, to heighten the horror. But tone must always *work with* content. Make sure the tone of your voice and the emotional resonance of each moment are blown with the same breath.

To Plot or Not to Plot

The world is God's novel, and people can't wait to find out what will happen next.

— I S A A C   B A S H E V I S   S I N G E R

When you think about plot, the first question you should ask yourself is: *How do I like to tell my stories?* Some writers, like Herman Melville and Dorothy Sayers, have a natural instinct for external dramatic events, those things that make readers want to find out: What happens next? Other writers, like James Joyce or Marguerite Duras, are more internal and also more interested in language, character, and imagery. Even in Joyce's short story collection, *The Dubliners,* which is fairly realistic, key events are introduced with great subtlety.

If you're the kind of writer who naturally thinks in terms of plot, then your voice and ability to plot are closely linked. You're gifted with a sense of a story's action, and can't imagine writing something without asking yourself: "What happens next?" You understand instinctively that a good plot functions like a series of billiard balls hitting against each other. You know how to get your story started and keep it going. And if you have a great plot and can work with character and language to make it interesting, you may be very lucky.

If you don't create plot naturally, you basically have two

choices: to forget about plot, or find ways to manipulate your voice so you can learn to work more effectively with a story's action. If you're writing short forms of fiction, the first choice may work, particularly if your stories are triggered by a sense of character, psychological complications, or more internal action. But most writers, unlike Joyce, can't depend on the strength of their imagery or ability to work with dialogue and character to carry a story. Usually, even very short fiction requires that something external "happen" to move the story forward.

Contemporary writers have a harder time finding material for externally generated plots than writers from earlier times. The Victorian world, for example, could have been designed by a plot-driven writer. There were all kinds of rules and restrictions in that era. Bastards couldn't inherit property and revelations about paternity and lineage could result in financial ruin. Married people were trapped because divorce wasn't allowed and extramarital sex was considered a great scandal. These rules created a world that was ripe with juicy, external secrets, secrets that could turn lives upside down if they were revealed. Within these confines, Victorian writers created extraordinarily well-plotted novels.

In this post-Freudian era, contemporary life is less restricted and in daily, ordinary life, there's less opportunity for scandal. It doesn't matter that much if Lord So-and-So wasn't your real father. It won't shock people if you have an affair. In the absence of external secrets, internal, psychological secrets have assumed more importance. This means that things often happen offstage, where action is internal, emotional. The center stage—a place where characters can engage with *each other* and not their inward revelations—is often used as a switchyard where characters meet to recharge their emotional batteries before scuttling back to the wings for private epiphanies and monologues.

I was made aware of this tendency in my own writing by a magazine editor who once said to me: "I'm not quite sure why you have this penchant for ending stories with the main character all by herself, caught in a moment of self-revelation." This was an eye-opener. After her question, I pushed my characters to confront each other, or avoid confrontations in interesting ways. I also introduced dramatic events in my stories, like illness, treachery, and even death. And I reread highly imaginative, vision-driven writers I admired like Kafka, Márquez, and Borges, with an eye to plotting. When I didn't allow myself to be dazzled by their imagery and use of language, I began to notice that their stories were heavily plotted, full of suspense, and often violent. Borges's penchant for violent, convoluted plots is startling, particularly in *Labyrinths*.

Kafka, too, relies on dramatic opening events which ricochet and create inevitable complications: *The Trial* begins with a man named K. being informed he's been accused of an unnamed crime. His search to discover his crime defines the action of the entire novel. In *Metamorphosis,* Gregor Samsa wakes up transformed into a dung beetle. After getting out of bed—with difficulty because he has to move all of his little legs—Gregor must decide whether to catch the commuter train to go to work. His decision not to leave the house in his horrific state leads to a series of inevitable catastrophes: Without his income, Gregor's family becomes poor and has to take in boarders. The family restricts Gregor to his room so the boarders won't notice him and leave. In spite of this injunction Gregor sneaks out one night to hear his sister play the violin. A boarder notices him, his father chases him back to his room, and hurls an apple that becomes embedded in his insect body. Neglected, wounded, Gregor eventually dies and is swept out with the garbage. A surreal story, yes. But hardly one without action.

If plotting doesn't come naturally to you, here are some things to try:

1. Be bolder about introducing dramatic external events. Start stories with what you think is the climax. Create a mystery or a secret that's external, not psychological. See what the characters do with it.

2. It's been said that there are only two plots in the world: "Someone goes on a journey," and "A stranger comes to town." (If you accept this model you probably have to concede that in modern fiction there are two nihilistic variations of these plots: "A stranger doesn't come to town," as in *Waiting for Godot,* by Samuel Beckett, and "No one goes on a journey," as in *No Exit,* by Jean-Paul Sartre.) Write two stories—one involving a journey, another involving the arrival of a stranger.

3. Scenes are found unities in fiction. They generally take place in one time, one place and show one continuous action. By the end of a scene a significant sense of transformation—or lack of transformation—has occurred. Work with tightening scenes. Learn to identify a scene and don't let it fizzle away without making sure that something—even a small transformation—happens that will influence the next scene.

4. Start a story with a dramatic event and allow that event to create a billiard-ball effect until the story reaches a dramatic conclusion. (Two hints: Don't end a story with a climatic event which should have happened toward the beginning, and avoid cluttering the beginning of your stories with unnecessary scenes.)

5. Plotting is often influenced by point-of-view. In the Rashomon model, for example, voices of various characters allow a story to come together puzzle-fashion, rather than in one long narrative flow, as Madison Smartt Bell did in *The Year of Silence*. In a novel with chapters that alternate third- and first-person voices, the plot may follow the same character but unfold with different nuances, as Margaret Drabble did in *The Realms of Gold*. Review Chapter Twenty-six, "Point of View," with an eye to plotting. Consider using a new approach to point of view to manipulate your plot.

6. Plot matters because human beings are eternally interested in "What happens next?" In daily life, this interest is manifested in gossip. Listen to gossip. Eavesdrop. Remember gossip you may have heard as a child. Write a story in which gossip between two people reveals an exciting secret. (Many stories have been built on the skillful use of gossip. Joyce's story, "The

Sisters," is a striking example. And Eudora Welty once said she got a lot of ideas for her stories by listening to what people talked about at the beauty parlor.)

Good writers use plotting so skillfully, you forget they're doing it. They bewitch you with characters, language, imagery, the range of their voice. Read these writers like a detective, noticing how they work with plot.

Sometimes finding a way to reframe ideas about plot gives you a fresh perspective—a way to tell yourself a new story about plotting—and this can help you read other writers creatively. For some reason, the "journey" and "stranger" theories of plotting delighted me—like a child with a new toy. With this in mind, I reread Poe's story, "The Masque of the Red Death," and had fun reframing it as a story about a stranger coming to town: Plague is raging in the surrounding area, but inside the castle noblemen dance and feast. Eventually they notice a figure in red with a mask among the dancers, and realize that the plague has come inside their castle walls. I also reread *As I Lay Dying* and saw it as an instance of someone going on a journey—but not a conventional one. Addie Bundren, the mother of the family, is dying, and her son Darl is building her coffin. The journey feels literal. She's leaving for another country. And her impending death creates suspense—which is amply justified. This kind of reading wasn't just an intellectual exercise. It gave me a new understanding of how writers handled plotting.

Plot is like oxygen. Most stories need it. But it's not everything. If it were, the crib sheet for Hamlet would be as good as the play. Dorothy Sayers is a wonderful mystery writer but the plots of her stories are enhanced by where things happen and who is doing them. In *Murder Must Advertise,* Lord Peter Whimsey goes to work for an ad agency and solves a murder, but what makes the book unique is the tone: It is a terrific satire on the world of business in the 1930s.

If plotting doesn't come naturally to you, the exercises we suggest here may not feel entirely "right" for your voice. But after a few false starts your voice may rise to the occasion and surprise you. You may write stories with tighter plots, stories that make readers ask, "What happens next?" You may also find you're creating more complications between characters and taking more risks with language and imagery. Plot is a structure that tends to challenge voice, pull it away from habitual modes, particularly in this post-Freudian world. By manipulating plot, the range of your voice may expand.

CHAPTER THIRTY-THREE

Gender Bending, Race Switching, and Beyond

I WAKE THINKING OF MYSELF AS A MAN

And as I rise slapping my feet
on the wooden floor
I begin to imagine myself
quite tall
with broad shoulders, a
painter who puts his feet
into dirty tennis shoes, does
not comb his hair and lumbers
largely into the kitchen, laces
loose in all this space.
I am this man, giant in my
female house, as I eat
my huge hands dwarf these bowls,
this breakfast!
I have become so big
I need a larger meal, more
eggs, coffee, and the newspaper
the newspaper rests like a
delicate letter in
my enormous grasp.
—SUSAN GRIFFIN, FROM
UNREMEMBERED COUNTRY

When voice is linked to the imagination, it can take you anywhere. Your voice is larger than a gendered self, or even a human self. Voice is capable of cross-dressing, of androgyny, of inhabiting a lake, a car. It comes from a place where categories of being lose their meaning, dissolve.

Spend a whole day imagining that you inhabit the body of a person of the opposite sex. Sit, walk, greet someone. Make love, talk on the phone. Get dressed. Watch people on the street. Read the paper. Cook and eat a meal. Fold laundry, fix a leaky faucet. Notice how you move and react, how simple acts are transformed. Notice what's on your mind, what rituals you keep. Write about one experience you had during this day from the point of view of your gender-switched persona.

Most often writers invent major, viewpoint characters in their own image. It's easiest. If you're a man in your fifties from Israel going through a midlife crisis, you feel most confident writing about an Israeli man in his fifties going through a midlife crisis. Biographical details may change, but the character is someone you can understand and imagine. Minor characters are seen through this man's eyes, just as you, the author, would view them. The world falls into place in a comprehensible way, like looking through a window.

But voice draws on more than personal biography, as any survey of literature shows. Consider: Caryl Phillips in *Cambridge* (a contemporary black man writing from the point of view of a white woman in the nineteenth century); Allan Gurganus in *Oldest Confederate Widow Tells All* (a gay white man writing in the voice of a ninety-nine-year-old white woman); Judith Guest in *Ordinary People* (a woman writing from the double point of view of a father and son); and Josephine Hart in *Damage* (a woman writing from the point of view of a sexually obsessed man).

Within every writer is a reservoir of imagination and feeling, fertile ground for cross-dressing. When people ask Josephine Hart if it was difficult to write like a man, she says, "Not at all.

This man came to me complete. I don't know what that says about me as a woman, but it was a complete act of symbiosis."

You may not realize until later what emotional impulse made you want to create a particular character. Styron says that looking back, he sees how many of his characters (Sophie, a troubled survivor of the Nazi camps, in *Sophie's Choice*; Nat, a rebellious slave, in *Nat Turner*) play out his own suicidal tendencies and spin toward depression. I suspect something else as well: that the details of these characters' lives allowed Styron to confront his own obsessions and inclinations in a profound way. Nazism and slavery provided the searing historical and personal circumstances that put his characters in a vise, skin to anvil with the same contradictions, terrors, and doubts that Styron wrestles with himself.

The projection of a trenchant facet of oneself onto a character is a primary impulse behind fiction. When this impulse drags your fictional inventions across lines of gender, race, ethnicity, or sexual orientation, you're in a fertile zone. Usually a vital part of yourself is speaking, a part that can be most fully accessed by taking on the persona of someone very different from your public self.

What does your voice return to over and over? Listen to your obsessions. Honor them, no matter how strangely they steer your stories. Your voice is truest when it howls from your uncensored inner self. As you draw on facets of yourself that are buried or marginalized in your daily life, you unleash the potent energy of your voice. It's an opportunity to let one of your buried personae emerge—perhaps a strong, masculine side if you're a woman, or a strong feminine aspect if you're a man. If you're as lucky as Josephine Hart, you'll be transported by the voice that claims your story. Listen to any voice in you that crosses gender or cultural lines. Become the person behind the voice.

As William Styron says, "A work of fiction should be able to attempt almost anything." Styron took enormous heat when he wrote *Nat Turner*. Attacked as being racist, accused of being presumptuous to believe he could understand the feelings of a slave, Styron was later awarded the Pulitzer Prize for this book. If he had surrendered to, the fear that he couldn't take on the character of a person different from himself, he would have shackled his creativity and his voice. Something powerful in him that was beyond race, beyond historical time, connected imaginatively with the characters of his story, and the novel lured the reader into believing.

The license to plunder your inner personae, the daring to reveal hidden aspects of yourself, is crucial to the full expansion and development of voice. The question is not whether you *can* inhabit the body and voice of a person of a different race, class, or sex from yourself, the question is whether you can do it convincingly.

Many writers do prodigious amounts of research before attempting to dress cross-culturally or otherwise. They read letters, diaries, and other primary source materials from the time period or culture they're writing about, as well as secondary sources. They immerse themselves in the speech rhythms, the diction, and the concerns of people like the characters they're creating. Even when you write close to home, this immersion can be essential. Ernest Gaines grew up in Louisiana, yet he spent months in Baton Rouge libraries doing research for *The Autobiography of Miss Jane Pittman,* to help revive the voices of his childhood. He needed to recall the speech of the people in the sugarcane fields, who said "mon" for mother, and called a porch a "gallery."

Emotions may be universal, but they're clothed in particulars. Keep a sharp eye to those particulars. And be realistic about your abilities of imaginative projection. Don't write about characters within whom you can't live and breathe. Even Styron admits he wouldn't have attempted Nat Turner's story if he hadn't grown up in the South.

GENDER BENDING

Only a few authors write across racial or cultural lines, but many at one time or another write across gender lines. With all the talk these days about gender and how men and women think and speak differently, we should be more sensitized than ever to gender differences. Capturing these differences in our characters is another matter.

A student of mine, a woman, wrote a story from the point of view of a man. Yet the story didn't feel generated by a man. Something eluded her, a particular way that this character thought or looked at the world that was different from the way she, the writer, did. Perhaps he'd think more about reroofing the house and less about the kid's runny nose. Or maybe he wouldn't think much at all, but would simply go get his hammer and nails.

To see whether you're truly living inside the skin of the man or woman you're impersonating, try gender switching. Take a story you've written that has both a man and a woman in it. Go through and make all the he's into she's, all the she's into he's. Then read it aloud. The result can be telling. You'll see the way you've projected gender differences, probably without even thinking about it. Now ask yourself: Do these gender distinctions reflect the characters you're trying to portray? Have you stayed too close to your own perspective?

Now take a first-person story narrated by a woman and read it as if the narrator were a man (or vice versa). What feels incongruous, silly, or off kilter? Rewrite the narration in the voice of the opposite sex and see what changes. Does the emotional landscape have a different feel, a different range? Do the details of scene shift? The focus of the story?

Gender switching can highlight your hidden assumptions about gender. It can push you to see how what we see, think, feel, and do *is* linked to gender, and it can also help you see the ways in which we sometimes operate on the basis of stereotypes. Convincing characters are always a bit of a surprise, but they're also people we can recognize.

Some more invitations to cross-dress and experiment:

1. If you're a man, go to a play area where there are a lot of mothers and children. Listen to the way the women talk, their rhythms, their choice of words, what they focus on, how they listen to each other. Find other gatherings of women (at a business lunch, at a coffee shop) and do the same thing. If you're a woman, find a gathering of men (at a bar, a baseball game, a party) and listen in the same way. Notice what distinguishes their speech patterns, what they talk about, how they listen. After you've listened for a while, write a monologue in the voice of a person of the opposite sex.

2. If you're a man, ask yourself: If I were a woman, what kind of woman would I be? How old? What occupation? What kind of family life? What would be my strongest personality trait? Write a diary entry from the point of view of this woman. If you're a woman, do the same thing, imagining yourself as a man. If you feel particularly daring, dress as this character and go about your day.

3. What part of yourself doesn't get expressed in your public persona? (You're a sociable, law-abiding person who goes to work, mows the lawn, and puts the kids' toys away at night, but secretly you're haunted by violent doubts and despair.) Create a character of a different sex, race, class, or ethnicity who embodies these hidden traits.

4. If you were to dress as your opposite, how would you appear? Write a fictional biography of your life.

5. Write a story from the point of view of an animal or insect, a house or a tree. Feel what it's like to inhabit this being or thing. Imagine how they experience the world around them.

CHAPTER THIRTY-FOUR

Unity: Discovering a Story's Design

I'm like a sort of living carpet. I need a pattern, a design. I come apart, I unravel, unless there's a design.

— REBECCA, A YOUNG WOMAN WITH
LEARNING DISABILITIES,
FROM *THE MAN WHO MISTOOK HIS WIFE
FOR A HAT*, BY OLIVER SACHS

A story is a complex tapestry, larger than its characters, dialogue, and sense of language. It has a total shape, a design, which readers grasp intuitively, beyond individual words and sentences. When the design is missing, no matter how many of these other elements are present, there still isn't a story. This is what Henry James meant when he once said, of a story, "I like it except for the whole thing."

Sometimes we call this elusive animal—this beast that gives a story shape—unity. When we say that a story has unity, we usually mean that the story feels complete, organic, and seems to have its own patterns of transformation. We also mean that when readers have finished reading the story, they have an intuitive grasp of a whole situation or stream of events. Everything seems to fit. Nothing seems extraneous. A reader may not know exactly what has happened, but the reader does know that *something* has happened. Even if the reader has to go back and reread the story for details, this sense of transformation is satisfying.

Unity isn't necessarily found in an exciting plot. Nor is it necessarily found in development of characters. Dino Buzzati and Rachel Ingalls offer relatively little in the way of character development but they write good stories, whereas many beginning writers have wonderful characters, but no story. Nor is unity always found in a vision of a cohesive whole, a continuous sense of time. Writers like Thomas Pynchon see the world as a jigsaw puzzle with many disparate parts yet readers still have a sense of a cohesive experience, which has been choreographed by the vision of the writer. Unity is alchemical—truly larger than the sum of its parts. It creates the illusion of life, right there on the page.

This aspect of a story is unique for every writer. It's linked to the way you make sense of life, see relationships, and weave them into a pattern—or even the lack of one. It's also linked to the way your voice works, particularly as the composer of the entire piece. For some writers the design comes easily. For others it's a hard-won commodity. And, for most writers, achieving unity in a story involves going through some emotional transformation *that is beyond issues of craft* and surprises them as they write the story. All writers—both seasoned and beginning—are, at some time in their career, plagued by work that has no unity. Stories may have beginnings and ends, but no middles. Middles but no beginnings. Characters but no dialogue. Often, and frustratingly so, there may be a series of compelling scenes that don't quite hang together. Or a chain of events that aren't choreographed by a persuasive vision. In each case what's lacking is unity, this sense of a story's total shape.

Particularly when you're learning to write, it can be hard to grasp the shape of a story until you've finished at least one draft. This is because voice often forges a story from one or two disparate elements—a haunting phrase, a single scene, a loquacious character, a sketchy plot, an intriguing title. These elements scatter on the page, and the voice of the story seeks to bind them. One might say that a writer often begins a story with a few trees, and later discovers the forest. The story's shape is what voice discovers, not what it starts out with.

For this reason questions about unity are most easily answered during revision. Sometimes it's premature to ask these questions in the middle of a first draft. If you feel stuck in the middle of a story, however, asking questions about unity can be useful. These are times when you don't know "what happens next," when everything you've written makes you feel trapped. This is a sort of hybrid phase. The embryo doesn't have a shape, but it may be possible to imagine its shape, or at least a few possible shapes, from the existing features. There are no rules for discovering unity in an unfinished story. But it often turns out that its seeds are contained in what you've already written.

In "Distilling Voice" (Chapter Eight) and "Inviting Accidents" (Chapter Nine), we encouraged you to use your deepest instincts to identify phrases and words that interested you, had resonance. Recognizing elements that help give a story unity involves identifying larger patterns, as well as homing in on words and phrases. These are still "interesting accidents" of voice, but may encompass whole scenes, characters, themes, imagery, dialogue. You're learning to identify whole sets, not just the elements inside them. Here are a few things to try, or some tips for finding the forest:

1. *Details* that seem insignificant at first later may become important and contribute to a sense of purposefulness. A doll, first described as one of many details in a room, is later discovered to hide valuable jewelry and this provides a climactic scene in your story. As the story unfolds, you may sense that other objects in the room of this story-universe aren't scattered randomly: A mirror may have a tarnished silver frame. The doll may be near a plate of old coins. Even though you may not have put them there consciously, these details foreshadow hidden treasure. When you get stuck in a story, consider keeping objects and details that interest you and discarding those that don't. See whether you can use whatever you keep to expand, sharpen, improvise, or create a pattern. For example, early in your story, the father bruises his son. This is a hint of anger. If you come to a place in the middle of your story and don't know "what comes next," you may be able to use this early hint and push the father's anger to more explosive possibilities. These details can be found everywhere—in dialogue, imagery, subtle actions, even in your characters' names.

   2.   A consistent *point of view* can provide a natural feeling of unity. If you have too many characters telling your story and begin to feel overwhelmed, try writing your story using the point of view of the character who most interests you. Or limit the point of view to two or three characters rather than six or seven. Or switch viewpoints between chapters, not within chapters.

   3.   *Minor characters* often contribute to a sense of unity when they populate a story in the service of a major character— usually by acting as a *mirror* or a *contrast* to the major players. Mrs. Reilly, the owner of a boarding house, is internally strong-willed, yet outwardly hesitant. She raises the rent in an apologetic voice and posts three "Wipe Your Feet!" signs on the front door in faint, wispy handwriting. You're not sure whether she belongs in your story at all until you realize that she mirrors the traits of the main character, Lars, who is one of her boarders. This may help you shape Mrs. Reilly to accent this aspect of Lar's character. Perhaps she and Lars butter bread the same way, applying lavish amounts with small furtive gestures. Or maybe they have long, overly polite discussions about how much money Lars owes for his long-distance phone calls to Sweden. When there's contrast between characters you can also use one character to underscore a character trait as well as subtly develop hidden aspects of character. Say you're writing a detective story in which the chief detective, Phil, acts chummy with neighborhood punks, doesn't miss one game during football season, and is generally streetwise; his partner, Ned, a minor character, always wears a tie to work and was educated at Harvard. As you begin to work with Ned, you realize that Ned is a key to one of Phil's secrets—he gave up a scholarship to help support his mother and has always resented his lack of education. Used in this way, minor characters, rather than seeming like neighbors who arrive at random, reinforce the themes and focus of the story. As you create minor characters, remember that they're not just stick figures. And if at some point you feel overwhelmed and confused by a profusion of characters, consider the following possibilities: 1) Get rid of a minor character who doesn't act as either a mirror or a contrast. 2) Collapse two minor characters into one. 3) Ask yourself if these minor characters are useful mirrors and contrasts in ways you haven't noticed, and develop the characters.

4. *Foreshadowing* always provides a sense that early actions and details are a doorway to the more explosive action of the story. Sometimes this is provided by small, specific details, like a tarnished mirror, old coins. At other times it's provided by action or specific scenes. (The first peck on the head by a single bird in an early scene of Alfred Hitchcock's *The Birds,* anticipates the full-scale bird attacks in the climactic scenes.) Once you know the high points of your story, you can search early scenes for details or incidents that may help set up the climactic scenes.

Sometimes you discover a foreshadowing event before you know the more dramatic scenes. I once wrote several drafts of a story that always stopped short after a scene in which two characters, turned on by sounds of lovemaking from the apartment below, make love on their kitchen floor. At some point I realized that this scene wasn't just an interesting bit of fluff. It was a scene that foreshadowed an explosive encounter. I allowed this scene to propel the action and was able to finish the story.

5. *Development of theme* is also a major source of unity, especially in a novel. Readers need a sense that all the details, characters, and actions ultimately help develop thematic strands. Notice what various images and events convey in your story: Is there a constant refrain of missed communication? A sense of the way characters undermine their own happiness? When you track the interesting tidbits that seem to have potential, take the opportunity to brainstorm and see what happens. Play with what interests you. Use these elements to search for a pattern.

Say you're writing a murder mystery in which four men,

former friends in the cattle business, tear into Baja California in souped-up four-wheel-drive vehicles. The mood is raucous and ornery. You know the men will suspect each other after the murder, but don't know yet who the murderer is, or why he does it. You've got a lot of scenes of drunken revelry and raunchy humor, but little sense of momentum. The story doesn't seem to be building the way it needs to.

Then you look back at a scene in which Leroy taunts Jackson for having eyes like a flounder, eyes that are too close together. You remember an earlier scene in which Jackson is able to see the pitted dirt road in the dark better than anyone else. You begin to brainstorm with this idea of unusual vision, night vision, think about shadows, mistaken identity, hat over the eyes, ace of spades. Gradually you suspect something new about Jackson: He's not who he seems to be. You move the story forward with new excitement, and as the men descend more deeply into the desert, you discover clues about Jackson's double life and what he's not telling his friends.

6. *Use of geography* as a spatial pattern can reinforce the plot or thematic movement of the story. (In *Heart of Darkness,* the action moves from an ordinary world into the heart of the dark, steamy jungle as the characters' darker sides are revealed.) Notice whether a pattern of movement through geography begins to emerge in your story. See whether there's a natural way to expand on this. How can this spatial movement work with the themes of your story?

7. A twist on the use of geography: *main characters who begin the story in separate spheres, and gradually come together.* The initial chapters of a novel may focus alternately on the lives of several characters—one in the high-rise business world of Los Angeles, one in the deserts of New Mexico, another driving cross-country from New York City. As the plot develops, these characters meet and their lives become intertwined. This provides a sense that the hodge-podge of early scenes are ultimately unified and are working in concert.

8. Reframe the notion of unity as *promises made to the*

reader, as well as to yourself. Scan your story for details, motifs, characters, particularly toward the beginning, and ask yourself how to thread them through your story. As a general rule of thumb, don't introduce elements at the beginning of a story or novel and drop them. Keep the original elements alive. Allow them to create significant transformations.

Unity is created by a sense that all pieces in the world of the story are contributing to the development of the plot and themes, that everything used is significant. You're looking for clues in the text itself, expanding some to their fullest possibilities, pruning others. Some writers learn to track their stories subliminally, others rely on more conscious dialogue. Over time, and with practice, it gets easier to think about a whole story while working on parts of it.

Returning to the Pressure Cooker

Stories often start with a sense of magic, but are rarely finished that way. As writers struggle to create unity and plot, they often describe reaching a stuck place, a point where they feel so boxed in, they can hardly breathe and have no idea of what happens next. Often this point precedes a breakthrough, or a complete rewrite. Others, however, describe long periods where they have no ideas at all. And most writers experience both kinds of frustration. Rilke heard the first lines of *Duino Elegies* in a burst of inspiration, but had to wait ten years to complete them. Part of this was due to the war, but part of it was that the *Elegies* arrived in fragments. Victor Hugo, on the other hand, was less patient: so he wouldn't leave his house to roam the streets of Paris, he made his valet lock up all his clothes and wrote wearing practically nothing. These are extreme examples. Yet they illustrate the conundrum writers face when they feel stuck: Do you push yourself? Or do you wait?

As you work over a period of time, you get better at knowing when to take a break and when you need to stick with what you're doing. And often you discover something surprising: In moments of supreme frustration, it sometimes helps to turn the pressure up rather than look for relief. Your work often revives when you return to the pressure cooker, that place of limited options we talked about in Chapter Nineteen. Here's an exercise for working with stringent restrictions in order to discover a scene's potential:

Pick one scene you're having trouble with and write it without allowing any external change in place or time and trying to avoid flashbacks. See if you can work with small, seemingly insignificant tensions in a scene, and don't end your scene until something is resolved. This may seem like obvious advice. Yet often when writers feel stuck in a story, they're tempted to do the opposite, like an insecure cook who uses too many spices to jazz up a meal. The subtle, growing tensions will be interrupted by a dramatic event, a change in time or place, a flashback, or a new character. Sometimes these devices work, but often they break the tension and scatter your story.

For example: Suppose I'm writing a story in which two owners of a construction firm are sitting in their trailer in Missoula arguing about what kind of second car to buy. One wants to buy a fancy sports car for meeting potential customers. The other wants to buy a pickup truck at the used car lot. The dialogue may be going well, and even revealing underlying tensions in their relationship. Suddenly I reach an impasse. It's tempting to skip a few beats at this point, have them decide to go out for beer, allow one of them to reminisce about his past as a race-car driver, or even have the phone ring, announcing they've won the lottery and have enough money to buy both cars. But in fiction, just like life, it's often subtle shifts that need to surface for a story to move forward. My best chances for sustaining tension will occur if I keep these men in their trailer.

If the action of a story is very internal and psychological, there are times when introducing something external helps to move the plot along. However, it must be an external event that escalates rather than dissipates tension. For instance, a neighbor might knock on the door and invite the partners to a poker party.

If they often argue about how to handle money, this invitation may push them into an explosive argument about whether to go to the party. This may lead you to your next scene.

Here are some more exercises for improvising with only a few potent elements of your story:

1. Go back to one important scene you've written and pick out only those images and events that leap out at you. Use them as central elements, strip away the rest, and rewrite the scene.

2. Go back to another important scene you've written for a story or novel-in-progress. Write the same scene, but make it twice as long. If the scene was three pages, make it six pages, without moving out of the scene. This may encourage you to expand the detail and dialogue and mine your material more deeply.

3. If you've been wandering endlessly through your story's maze, writing scene after scene, feeling directionless, write your story in three scenes. Write the last scene first, then the one before that, then the scene before that. This will force you to focus on what's at the heart of your story.

4. If you've had many false starts on a story or novel, take from each foray at least one prize—something that still speaks to you: the central attitude of a character, a key image. Use it in something new.

View your false starts and dead ends as opportunities, not failures. In this messy business of writing, everything you do is valuable. You never know what you might want to salvage later, even if it's only a phrase, a character. (Stephen King's wife rescued his novel *Carrie* from the wastebasket!) Mixed in with the dead rhetoric and directionless rambling are those inkblots of raw voice that can lead you somewhere exciting—if you let them.

Once, in the Yucatan, I crawled through the narrow, sweaty passages of a Mayan temple toward the sacred chamber at the center. Inside that chamber, the guidebook said, stood a stone jaguar with two piercing jade eyes. The twisting stairways, barely shoulder-width, were choked with tourists, the stone slippery to the touch. The humid air stuck in my lungs. I felt suffocated. I wanted to turn back. But even more, I wanted to see that sacred chamber and those jade eyes. I knew it would be worth the discomfort. And it was.

Remembering this has sometimes helped me stay with stories and trust my voice when the going gets hard. At other times I know I have to take a break. I often realize this when I'm making busywork for myself in the story—doing endless line editing, for example, or letting my inner critic have a field day telling me I haven't done enough research. Sometimes all I need is a short break. I go for a run, read the paper mindlessly, prowl around my garden, and I'm ready to begin again. Sometimes the break is longer. I put the story in my desk drawer and let it age for a while.

Whether you decide to take a break or forge ahead, at some point your story or novel usually kicks back into motion. Sentences come. New scenes emerge. The plot unravels. You discover the sacred room. However, very few stories or novels get written in one draft, and your voice is honed most completely in revision.

Revision

Revision: Exploding the Myth

Revision is perhaps the greatest improvisational challenge for the writer: You must return to the original dream of your story (a concept originally formulated by John Gardner) and change parts of the dream so seamlessly, they'll appear as though they've always been there. In a sense you must become an impeccable thief when you revise, entering a room quietly, adding a piano here, removing an armchair there, and doing it so skillfully, that the occupants don't notice. To accomplish this, you have to allow your voice the same freedom you allowed it when you started the story. You have to be willing to be surprised by unexpected images, different significant events, strange characters. You may even decide that you have to write a different story. This is a creative process, as creative as the first draft of a story.

Few of us have this approach to revision when we start to write. We tend to think of revision as a neat mechanical process in which the writer pastes, prunes, grafts, incorporating various suggestions: If an editor says she wants to know what a character looks like, you dutifully add a description of a face. If a friend says a certain middle-aged man would never sell chickens for a living, you take out a vibrant, descriptive passage and substitute a labored flashback. But stories are organic entities, and your voice is their life-giving substance. If you add a passionless description of a face, it will sound all wrong and the passages around it will exude antibodies—just like a failed organ transplant. Similarly, if you subtract something crucial, the story feels amputated. The task in revision is the same as in writing a first draft—to find the path that leads from ideas about the story to the voice that will tell the story.

Unfortunately, editors and teachers, as well as writers themselves, unwittingly reinforce the myth that revision is a logical process that can be accomplished quickly by artificial manipulation. In their eagerness to offer helpful suggestions, in their desire to do something right away, they forget that just as raw voice led you into your story, raw voice will lead you into revision. This process of reactivating voice can be encouraged, but it can't be controlled, and it certainly can't be engineered by outside manipulations or the logical, discursive mind. Without the vitality of spontaneous voice, good revisions can't happen.

How do you accomplish this reconnection with voice? This question often stymies writers. A story that felt exciting when you started it becomes flat and uninteresting when you read it over—and perhaps untenable after getting feedback from someone else. You can't imagine what you're going to do with any of the suggestions you've received. You don't want to work on the story, ever again. Alternately, you have tangible and exciting ideas for a new scene, but when you incorporate them, there are no sensate details and the scene feels like a dull synopsis.

When you hit this sort of low, it's important to remember that by returning to raw, reenergized voice you'll circumvent a lot of problems (including following false leads as a result of misguided advice) and eventually find your way back into your story. This is a simple principle that you may have to remind yourself of again and again because the desire to rush in and fix a story by sheer force is very powerful.

Revision is a deeply personal matter. Everyone has a slightly different channel back to raw voice, and everyone requires different conditions to revitalize it so you can go back into a particular story and improvise. For some people a return to the energized tidbits that are scattered throughout a first draft renews excitement about the material. For others it's sheer fury that a draft isn't working. For some it's a result of simply putting the manuscript away for a couple of months—or a serendipitous accident that gets you to see the material in a new way. (More than once, a draft I'm transferring from my studio wastebasket into the garbage bin has caught my eye and pleasantly surprised me.) You may have to go through a long process of trial and error to discover what conditions reenergize your voice. And these conditions may change from story to story. It's crucial to remember that there isn't any formula.

As a general rule, most writers need to develop a receptive curiosity toward their stories. When a story isn't working, it's helpful to take a few deep breaths, put aside editors, inner critics, and other innumerable voices, and remember what it was that originally excited you. Was it a pattern of light on your bedroom floor? A dream of a large black book with a cracked spine, full of scientific formulas? The vision of a character who envies her husband's dreams? Go back to these images, sit with them, and then put the story away for a while. This receptive attitude toward your own work can be the beginning of reactivating voice.

As you revise, you must work to discover the conditions that reenergize voice. This may involve learning how to work with the material (for instance, you discover that writing down free associations and impressions about the story helps you get new ideas). Or it may involve learning how to work with yourself (for instance, you find out that it's best to wait a month before reading over a final draft). Your job here is to reactivate your raw voice in a more focused way, to discover your point of entry back into the story. You may ultimately rewrite the whole story from scratch, but you may also revise using many elements from your original draft. This means that you're improvising within restrictions and limitations that you have previously set up.

IMPROVISATIONAL TRAINING

Revision is just one more step in improvisational training. For most artists, improvisation almost never means being completely spontaneous. When a blues pianist does a riff, what sounds like pure invention is partly the result of years of practicing scales, chords, runs, and beats until they've become second nature. In a moment of pure inspiration, the pianist calls up what's needed to create new patterns. If he's good, you hear a surprising and satisfying rearrangement of notes. But there's history to the surprise and lots of work behind it.

Like musicians, writers must practice their craft. This happens as a result of working with raw voice, as well as by simply writing and writing a lot. Over time, you begin to recognize and identify how your voice organizes itself into larger patterns, the "interesting accidents" of scenes, dialogue, developments of plot. Over time, you begin to learn your own patterns so well, that when you're in the middle of a story and "make something up," you tend to choose material that leads you deeper into your story. The more you trust your improvisational abilities, the more you can relax and let voice do its work.

The word "revision" usually implies that the writer has written at least one complete draft of a story. Many writers do. But not everyone writes a story by finishing one draft and going on to another. One writer I know spends a few hours doing freewrites each day, expecting no results. Most of the time nothing happens. Every few weeks, however, a freewrite spontaneously becomes a story which she finishes in one sitting and rarely needs to revise. Another writer describes her first draft as a "screen" for her real story. This draft is usually rhetorical, bereft of dialogue and imagery. She throws it away and at some point writes what she calls "the real" story. Other writers stare at fragments for a long time until patterns coalesce and there's a sense of something "happening" instead of a collection of words. And some writers stop halfway through the story—either because they are interrupted or they can't figure out how to continue. In these cases, the original impulses of voice must be recovered even before a first draft is finished.

The secret of revision is to ignite the original fictional dream, reactivate your raw voice, and discover your point of entry back into your story. We'll discuss ways to do that in the following chapters.

The Art of Reading Your Own Fiction

The first stage in any revision process is usually reading over whatever you've written, whether it's a chapter of a novel, a short story, or a fragment. Reading your own work ought to be simple. You sit down with a pencil, maybe with a cup of tea or coffee, and read. Yet a surprising number of writers fail themselves and their work so badly at this stage that many wonderful first drafts never get past the first reading.

Reading a draft can be painful. You may have written in ecstasy. You may have thought you were writing the story of the decade, perhaps the century. But now you're considering the work as a whole, and this can be a shock—like looking in a mirror in full sunlight on a day when you haven't shaved, or gotten any sleep. The impulse is to rush in and start to scribble and cross out—just as you'd want to scrub and comb and spruce up. Don't! Just read. If you start to make changes at this stage you won't get a chance to grasp the story as a whole. You'll become lost in questions of style, language, and diction and miss what you're looking for.

What are you looking for? You're looking for significant

events, elements that crackle, irritate you, puzzle you, and—most of all—excite you. You're looking for what you remember, hours after reading, perhaps at two in the morning when you wake up and think, *that character is always wearing a red blouse; she's always looking out the window. . . .*

You're also listening for language and cadences that excite you. You're reading with your ears as well as with your eyes.

This process is similar to the process we suggested in the chapters called "Distilling Voice" and "Inviting Accidents," where you read over a freewrite, looking for interesting accidents of language or image. The story probably hasn't appeared yet. But there are clues, signs, talismans—incidents that have further potential, lines of dialogue that reverberate. You're hunting.

You're also looking for unity—the mysterious glue which holds a story together. You're looking for things that can be lopped off—tangents, unnecessary details, dead ends—as well as things that are essential but haven't been fully expanded or used. Elimination of unessentials and expansion of essentials is a key to creating a sense of unity. (In the next chapter, you'll meet another ally, the story editor, who can help you with this question.)

Although this process of reading and rereading isn't actually writing, it's very important work. You're engaged in an odd kind of brooding, a stance of active receptivity. Most important, you're allowing yourself to have a direct experience of your story. Without such an experience, it's hard to develop a working relationship with an early draft, and without a working relationship you'll never have the heart to revise. In this stage, you're getting to know your own story—mulling things over, learning certain lines by heart, noticing odd repetitions. You may read your draft a number of times, perhaps even over a period of weeks, before any sort of rewriting strategy crystallizes.

T I P S F O R R E R E A D I N G

Here are some things to remember when you're rereading a first draft:

1. Don't start to make stylistic changes right away. Instead, read as if your body were a Geiger counter, and you're scanning for ore. Register those places where, as you read, you feel a reverberation, excitement, or energy in your body—perhaps by marking a pencil line down the side of the page where you hear a buzz, not marking where you don't. Make a light mark in the margin, almost as if tracing a graph, and keep on reading. Sometimes it helps to think of a first draft as a musical score. Once more, you're training your ear, listening for awkward voice shifts, musical resonance, and false notes.

2. If you're the kind of writer who responds first to what's wrong with a story, honor that instinct. Make a similar mark in the margin when you come across things that irritate you, that sound wrong. Listen for music that doesn't sing, shifts in voice that feel abrupt.

3. Even if you can't stand a draft by page three, give your draft the courtesy of reading it all the way through. A first draft is an important offering. If it doesn't contain treasures (and chances are it will contain at least one), it usually represents the first layer of an archaeological dig. You can't discover the sacred room without it. Treat your draft with respect, and treat the writer who wrote it with respect. Even if you're very disappointed, consider it an important effort, a portent for the future.

4. Cultivate patience. It may take weeks, even months, to know what to do with some drafts. Knowing *that* something is wrong is different from knowing how to fix it. Don't try to figure things out too quickly. Live with the frustration and the problem.

5. Remember that no amount of manipulation can call forth the will to reenter the dream of the story. Understanding craft can help you pinpoint areas of risk and tension. But once you start reworking, voice has to take over. (For example, say you notice that two characters have a very boring conversation. You might decide, deliberately, to have them talk about something very risky. An intellectual understanding gets you to this point. But then you have to lose control, allow yourself to improvise, and see what happens.) Therefore, when you identify a problem, try to resist mechanical, artificial solutions. Trust that when you get back to the story you'll be able to improvise.

6. Have faith that whatever prompted the original inspiration is still there and that the story is waiting to be told. Few writers start stories without a good reason, and usually the inspiration can be revived. (The only time this isn't the case is when you write a story that you think you should write—a story that didn't come from the heart.) If you were excited by a story once, you will be again. Be willing to wait to revise until you feel the excitement.

7. It's also extremely helpful to read your story out loud, listening for false notes. The spoken voice doesn't lie. When you trip over words, stumble over certain sentences, it's a clue: You may have abandoned your natural voice for an affected voice, and camouflaged truth in the process. You may be skipping over a scene, or including a flashback that doesn't feel urgent. If you prefer to read your work by yourself, read out loud alone, or into a tape recorder, marking the places where your spoken voice seemed to resist the written word. If you feel comfortable sharing your work, find a friend and read your draft aloud. The friend needn't comment on the work. All he or she has to do is listen. Reading work out loud is advice that writers often give to each other yet often forget to follow themselves. It's one of the most helpful ways to grasp the rhythm and shape of your story, the authenticity of dialogue, the passages with authority. Do it!

Should Dick Have a Beard?:
Meeting Your Editors

You, the writer, are the one who revises—the one who reaches back to raw voice to reenergize and deepen your story. Yet in this process you're guided by your inner editors: parts of yourself that know how to listen to a draft, and how to coach the story along. These inner editors share their insights, then get out of your way so you feel free to return to raw voice, to improvisation, and to passion.

Experienced writers work with these inner editors so intuitively, they hardly know they're there. The signals between editor and writer flash almost imperceptibly. But if you're still developing rapport with this part of yourself, as most writers are, it's useful to think of your inner editors as personae: distinct characters with different personalities and histories. As you meet and get to know them, you'll discover how best to work with them and become adept at spontaneously using their wisdom. The more you work with them, the more they'll disappear into your writing.

MEETING YOUR EDITORS

"Make Maritza less sentimental." "Take out that sentence." "Cut the dachshund." Inside the cacophony of advice that clamors in your head as you reread are essentially three kinds of editors—the story editor, the sentence editor, and the detail editor—and it helps if you can learn to tell them apart. Each has distinctive characteristics; you'd never mistake them in a crowd. And each has his place in the process of revision.

The story editor takes the long view. She steps back to look at the story as a whole. She notices whether your story maintains dramatic tension and momentum, and whether it takes the reader somewhere. She makes sure you haven't missed any important dramatic opportunities. She's unconcerned about the fact that the vase on the mantel in scene one is pink, but in scene two is blue (unless this detail is crucial to the story), but she gets very upset if a major character remains undeveloped. She's most irate when bored. The cardinal sin, to her, is to write a story that doesn't make the reader want to keep reading.

The sentence editor is a musician with language, a master of style. Words are his music, and he listens with a finely tuned ear to their rhythm and cadence. He hears the stiffness in the sentence, "The corn stalks were a crisp brown and stirred and rustled slightly," and the musicality when it's changed to "The corn stalks, crisp and brown, stirred and rustled." He hears the flat spots, the easy phrases, the lack of variation in sentence structure. He hears voice shifts: places where the voice is direct and trustworthy, and places where it becomes stilted or dishonest. He's able to point out rough spots in your writing and help you sharpen them.

His distant cousin, the detail editor, walks through the story with a magnifying glass. He gets riled if Juanita stops along Calle Agua to take a heady sniff of the irises because he knows that irises don't have an aroma. And he worries incessantly about subject-verb agreement or whether you've checked your German phrases for accuracy (maybe you'd better spend another week in the library). He gets upset if Dick, the psychiatrist in your novel, has a beard, because he happens to know (his brother is a psychologist) that psychologists usually have beards, but not psychiatrists.

The detail editor is a bit obsessive: No editor is going to reject your story because Dick didn't shave. But when your story is done, the detail editor will have some wise offerings to help make your story shine.

There's actually a fourth kind of editor, an amalgam of these three, who can also appear. He's aligned with the inner critic, and is often a combination of voices: your parents, your teachers, well-meaning friends, fellow writing students. He talks about anything that concerns him: "That character is too depressing." "You need to explain your slang." His voice is intimidating and full of himself. If you listen to him too much, he steals your authority, and interrupts your relationship with your own work and voice.

This really isn't an editor at all, but your inner critic in the guise of an editor, trying to sound helpful, but actually stifling your instincts and voice. He comes in at moments when you're detached from your material, when your own intuitive relationship to your work is weakened. To ban him from your repertoire of editors, you simply need to cultivate your own relationship to your work, and trust your sense of what you're trying to do. You may need to stop showing your work to an overly critical friend, or drop out of a writing group that doesn't make you feel good about what you're doing.

To get a better sense of these editors, try visualizing them. What does your story editor look like? What about your sentence editor? Your detail editor? Your inner critic? What is each one wearing? How do they talk? What kind of office does each have? Sit them down at a table and let them argue about how much they should get paid and why. You might also want to have a conversation with each of these editors. Tell them what you want from them, and what you don't want them to do.

WHO'S ON FIRST

If you were to probe the story of your inner editors' lives, you'd find some interesting biographical nuggets. For instance, the detail editor is short-lived. He enters when the story is done (or nearly done), points out a few errors of logic or fact, and disappears. His life and the life of the story don't coincide a whole lot: He's part of the clean-up crew.

The sentence editor is a lively presence, eager to step in as soon as the first sentence is on the page, busily fiddling with grammar and syntax. Because she's eager to speak up and easy to hear, there's a temptation to listen to the sentence editor too soon. Be careful here: In early drafts, the sentence editor's desire to polish may interrupt the spontaneous flow of voice. If the sentence editor is too active, you may never hear the story. Also, the sentence editor is too easily allied with the inner critic; the sentence editor can become very picky about language, making you feel you can't write. Later, after you've worked with the story editor, the sentence editor is an important ally. But initially, her desire to fix and fiddle needs to be held in check.

It's the story editor whose presence is most crucial to revision, and who is around the longest. She emerges first in the rereading process and is a constant companion as you're bringing your story to life. She has the ability to recognize where voice is energized, and *to energize voice herself.* This is the quality you most need and trust from any of your inner editors. For this reason, she's the one you want to listen to first.

Listening for the Story Editor

I was writing a scene in which a husband and wife come home late at night to their dark house. They go into the bedroom and the wife slips off her belt and shoes. The room is lit by a half moon. She's struck by the milky blue of her husband's shirt in the pale light. It's hypnotic, and she reaches to touch it. They make love.

Blegh. The scene was too predictable, dull.

I read the scene over. Something about the way she fingered his shirt intrigued me. I went back to that moment and began to write spontaneously. Suddenly she dropped her blouse and underwear to the floor and slipped his cotton shirt over her bare skin. She went to the doorway, stepped onto the cold concrete porch. Above her, moonlight slivered through the olive tree. She was feeling lit up, strangely androgynous. A surge of power ran through her, a power over her husband she hadn't known before. The story took a new, more original direction.

My story editor had stepped in to get me to pay attention to a detail I might have glossed over. My imagination had offered an opening. That shirt glistened. "Listen," my inner editor said. "There's something exciting here."

Your voice and your story editor are symbiotic. It's hard to know where one ends and the other begins. The story editor knows how to take a backseat while your voice is improvising. And she knows how to step in when needed with an intuitive hint about your material, or an element of craft. She's like a conductor, counting time, humming along, but only interrupting when your phrasing is off, or your rhythm too slow. "Speed up there!" "More feeling!" Most important, she works not only with what's on the page, but with you, the writer: Her insights call forth your imagination and passion. She invites you to stretch out, tell her more.

Here's what she might ask:

1. Where is the story most energized, riveting? What part of the story sticks with you after you've put it down?

2. Did you feel dramatic tension and momentum *throughout* the story—that sense that you want to keep turning the page and find out what's going to happen next? If not, where in the story were you bored, or where did you feel the energy lag?

3. Does the tone of the voice grab you, hold your interest? Does it feel right for the story you're telling?

4. Does the point of view feel right for the story?

5. Did you sense any missed opportunities in the story (characters that are not developed, complications in relationships that are hinted at and then seem to vanish, scenes that are hurried, intriguing details that are introduced but not used)?

6. Do you sense any risks not taken (conflicts between characters that are set up then backed away from, dangerous plot turns that have been modified, outrageous behavior that has been toned down, dialogue that has been made polite)?

7. Did the story have a sense of unity? Did all details, scenes, and characters contribute to the story's plot and themes? Were any details, scenes, or characters extraneous, redundant, or unnecessary?

8. Was the dramatic action pushed to its furthest point of tension? Did you feel the story stopped short of where it could go?

9. Did you feel that the story took you somewhere? Do you have the feeling that *something happened*? Do you have the feeling that it was *about something that mattered*?

10. Does the story remain with you after you put it down? Does it have an afterlife in your emotions, body, mind?

Dialogue with the Story Editor

All writers carry on a dialogue with the story editor as they work. This dialogue is a way of talking to the self, checking in, working in tandem with your voice. The story editor is a part of yourself that can detach and work outside of voice. Yet she doesn't interrupt voice. She's a linchpin or passageway between objectivity and subjectivity. Your voice gains training from her, and after you've listened to her for many years, she becomes a part of you, a part of your voice.

How do you develop this story editor? You've been doing it all along, as you've experimented with voice, paid attention to its energy and worked to train your ear. In the early stages of your work with voice, you were listening for an off-key note. Now you're listening in a more complex way to the total dynamic of your story, to the way all the parts—character, plot, tone, point of view—work together.

In Chapter Thirty-seven we suggested you reread a story you'd written as the first step in revision. As you responded to those parts that excited you and those parts that lagged, you were developing a relationship with your story editor. You were listening to the story as a whole and recognizing what was extraneous, stilted, dry—and what was alive. Here's a way to take that exercise further.

Take a story you've written, or a chapter of a novel, and read it in one sitting, without interruption. As you read, quickly mark the places in your story that feel strained, or where your writing feels labored, or your attention strays. Now take these passages out and reread your story. You may be surprised at how unnecessary those parts were. Or how easy it is to slip in a line of dialogue to convey what a long passage did.

Now read through another story or chapter of a novel, but this time mark all the places where you feel excitement. Listen for where a character does something unexpected, or a small detail leaps out at you. Ask yourself some questions about that detail, action, or image. For example, you may notice that a couple of times in your story a character is caught glancing in a mirror. Ask: What feeling does she have when she looks in the mirror? What is she looking for? What doesn't she want to see? Try to discover what this detail tells you about your character or story line, and let these insights guide the action of a new scene, or shift the action of a previous one.

The story editor is particularly good at helping you mine your material more deeply, and discover things about your characters you hadn't known. And she's a great resource to call on when you're stuck. I was working with a scene in which a fiftyish man, upset because his fifteen-year-old daughter had begun not coming home at night, went to talk to a woman friend, Anna. He was pacing Anna's living room, ranting. "She's crazy. These kids think they can do whatever they want. If I didn't come home at night my father'd be waiting at the door, smacking his belt in his fist." I thought I was getting all the right nuances of this man's speech and emotions: the hidden rage at his father, the feelings of losing control of his daughter. Yet the dialogue seemed to float. I didn't believe it.

From the side curtains I heard a voice coaching me: motivation! Why had his outrage sent him *here,* to this woman's newspaper-strewn rug? He wanted something from her. Sympathy—something more. He wanted her to criticize his wife, to blame her. He wanted Anna to gaze at him with the understanding his wife wasn't giving him. *He wanted her to find his desperation exciting.*

As soon as I realized this, his dialogue became anchored to Anna, the room, his own forbidden desires. He stopped ranting. His voice became subdued. "Maybe I'm the one who's crazy," he said. He slumped to the floor, leaned against Anna's knees. The story editor knows that what your character wants can instantly ground a scene, and channel voice.

If you work more intuitively, here's another way your story editor can help you: The voice from the sidelines can throw out key words that open up a provocative direction. The man is pacing, saying, "She's crazy. These kids think they can do whatever they want. . . . " Your story editor coaches him with the words: "Home." "Sex." "Loneliness." He stops in the middle of the rug, says, "Marla should've been home more. All those damn meetings she goes to." It's his wife he's angry with, his wife who's disappointed him.

These nudges from the story editor can get you off automatic and into that passionate place of spontaneous knowing. When Frances Ford Coppola was filming *Apocalypse Now* in the Phillipines, he had no idea how the story was going to end. He was paying Marlon Brando a million dollars a week for three weeks of work, was way over budget, and desperate to finish the film. Cameras whirring, Brando paced his jungle cave, bald and hulking. As Coppola coached him from the sidelines ("Why are we in Vietnam?"), Brando struggled to improvise, intoning, "It's our time to grab this moment in history. It's our time to . . . to teach . . . I can't think of anymore dialogue today." How they finally came up with the ritual slaughter that ended the movie as Brando gasped those famous last words, "the horror, the horror," was a matter of luck (Coppola just happened to watch some Philippine villagers slaughter a water buffalo), tenacity, and a willingness to stumble and improvise.

Fortunately, your characters are not as expensive as Coppola's were. You can afford to take your time pushing them, playing around. You may have a lot of false starts. You may feel like you're groping. But you can develop a quiet voice that stands outside your character as an imaginative guide, willing to push, willing to try something different.

These exercises call on your story editor to observe, intuit, and push your voice forward. You can use the list of questions offered in this chapter to prompt more dialogue with your story editor. But don't rush yourself, or feel overly anxious. You'll continue developing your story editor over time, as you read other writers, take a class, join a workshop, and keep writing.

Read widely. Read authors you love, those you despise, and those you can't relate to. Read authors from different cultures, the opposite sex. Read a story about something you would never write about. Join a workshop and listen to the drafts of other writers. You'll hear surprising things. (Oh, he just jumped into a new scene; he didn't explain what happened in between.) By learning to listen to other people's stories, you'll learn to listen to your own. Over time, your ear will become more discriminating, and you'll hardly notice your story editor at work.

Listening for the Sentence Editor

You have to be able to do two things to write a story: You have to be able to write, and you have to be able to tell a story. The sentence editor knows how to recognize good writing. She has an ear for pacing and cadence. She understands how language conveys emotion: where the sentences need to be sharp, abrupt; where they can be more leisurely. She hears where sentences are awkward, cumbersome. And she hears where voice is immediate and sensory.

The sentence editor has the powerful ability, too, to pick out imposter voices. Her ear catches those phrases that are distanced, generalized, overly rational: "Randy worried about the pace of his career development." She can hear the voice that is gripped by logic, that hasn't given over to the wild and passionate force of raw voice. Like voice teacher Iris Warren, she can hear the phrases that are tinny, that come from the throat only, that aren't belted from the diaphragm, the gut.

Here are some of the things she listens for:

1. Are any sentences distanced, generalized? Can they be made more sensory, immediate?

2. Are any sentences forced, overly clever, too ornate? Can they be written more simply?

3. Are the sentences wordy? Can any words or phrases be cut? Can whole passages be cut?

4. Do the prose rhythms reflect the emotional content—for example, if the emotion is breathless, impassioned, do the rhythms of the language convey this? (But watch out: There are no rules here. Clipped phrases can suggest ennui and lassitude, or urgency—depending on how they're used. Dispassionate, journalistic sentences can convey terror.)

5. Does the action feel mechanical, as if the writer were giving stage directions (she stood up, she sat down, she looked up, she walked over)? Can a more resonant voice be called forth to elicit atmosphere, mood, detail of character, emotion?

6. Do individual words evoke and describe? Are certain words used too often?

7. Are any sentences clichéd? Can the language be made more original?

8. Are there places where you hear blatant shifts in tone (a passage that was vivid and sensory lapses into explanation; emotionally forceful language is followed by cerebral language)?

9. Is the sentence structure repetitive and unimaginative? Can it be varied?

10. Are there too many adjectives or adverbs? Can some be cut?

To work with your sentence editor, you need a good ear. The sentence editor, like the story editor, begins by listening. Rather than listening for the whole sweep of the story, though, the sentence editor pays close attention to individual sentences and paragraphs. Read your story aloud once again. Notice where the voice feels fluid, natural. And notice any sentences that sound heavy, any places where the rhythm is stilted.

If you've found some places where your voice feels strained, instead of sitting down and rewriting, try improvising a new passage out loud. Your spoken voice, especially when you stop listening in on yourself, can often connect you with a more natural way of speaking. Pace the room as you speak, and feel the language in your body. Try using your spoken words as the basis for a new passage.

Another way to rework those wooden passages your ear has noticed is to write quickly, in the dark, with your eyes closed. Use sentence fragments. Let yourself drift into a semihypnotic state. Perhaps do some freewriting or nonsense writing as a warm-up. You may be surprised by the way language roils up.

As we've suggested before, it's also good practice to read the work of your favorite authors out loud. Listen to the voice as you would listen to a musical score. Notice the phrasing, tone, cadence.

DIALOGUE WITH THE STORY EDITOR

If a story is nearly complete, the sentence editor does fine-tuning: cutting unnecessary language, making a few sentences more direct. But if a story is still developing, the sentence editor often works in collaboration with the story editor. Sometimes these two editors seem to meld into one powerful reader of your work.

By reading the surface of the water a good sailor knows what the sea is like underneath. He knows there's an important interplay between surface and depth. The sentence editor can use his surface readings as clues for working with the story: The sentence editor hears a false note—a place where the language is stiff, too cerebral, out-of-character, forced—and alerts the writer that a character is expressing a shallow emotion. The writer can dive back into that dramatic moment, and live in the character's skin more directly.

As an example, here's a student's story about a woman who escaped to a city-run shelter after being battered by her husband.

We knew nothing more about her at the end than we did at the beginning.

> *Her right eye was swollen shut with a smear of deep-purple bruise. Her lower lip was torn, scratches covered her face. She wore a pink three-quarter length jacket zipped up to her chin, with a brown stain over her left breast, and old running shoes.*

These beginning sentences are spare but detailed. We see the woman's purple-blue bruise, her spotted jacket. By the middle of the story, though, the sentences become more distanced, abstract. The narrator starts to summarize.

> *During that time our young guest nervously resumed the routine she had developed since coming to us, but she never talked and always seemed on edge. I could also tell that she was suffering some of the early effects of pregnancy—nausea and fatigue—as well as the ongoing aches and pains caused by her beating. Nevertheless, she was industrious. She helped with cleaning chores as well as with cooking.*

Reading these lines, it's the sentence editor who hears the shift in voice, from immediate to distanced, from specific to abstract. But it's the story editor who takes the cue and realizes that this middle part of the story moves too quickly. There's more to explore. The writer shifts to a more immediate, sensory voice. The pregnant woman is peeling potatoes in the kitchen, leaning weakly against the counter. A long-faced woman sucking cherry Life Savers heaves a pan onto the stove and says to her, "I saw that guy hanging out front again last night. Just staring at your window." The pregnant woman tenses, and a more detailed scene emerges.

This collaboration between the sentence and story editors works in the other direction, too. The story editor may feel the potential for excitement and transformation in the plot, and alert the writer to reach for a faster pace, a more urgent tempo. The writer reshapes the languid sentences into staccato, or cuts the superficial gab and lets her characters rip. The writer may be working with sentences, but he's guided by the insights of the story editor.

Writers who are most sensitive to language, who have access to a powerful and sophisticated sentence editor, sometimes have a harder time finding narrative. Like poets, they work in relation to what they hear and don't think much about story. They easily write resonant paragraphs, original images, but they struggle to weave these images into a whole. And often writers who are great storytellers, who know how to create a riveting plot, have more difficulty listening to the musicality of language. They've got a great story, but rather mediocre sentences. The writing feels stiff, lacking the potent energy of raw voice. These writers need to learn to get their sentence editor and story editor to communicate, use one as the cue for the other.

The Timing of Revision

One secret of revision is timing—timing that helps you find the entrance into your original dream and connects you to spontaneous voice. Most writers need some sort of time lag between finishing a draft and going back into the material, and writers have different rhythms. You may work quickly, returning to a story immediately, fired up. Or you may need six months, a year, or even five years. Revision can take a while. Some writers need their stories to sit for years, like slow-rising loaves of bread.

If you happen to require lengthy intervals between drafts, and are just starting to write, it may be a while before you work out a successful rhythm for revision. (My own rate is so slow that for the first eight years of my writing career, I didn't believe I could revise at all.) In the process of learning your own rhythm, you may endure false starts and disappointments. But take heart. Revision is often where you learn the nuts and bolts of your craft and begin to develop an intelligent dialogue between your empathic inner editor, who tracks your story, and your voice, who tells your story. Even if a revision fails, you may find that you incorporate your experiments in a new story. For example, after years of writing and rewriting clunky dialogue in unsuccessful revisions, my characters finally began to have spontaneous conversations.

Just as writers know when they're ready to start a story, they usually know when they're ready to revise. Trust your apathy; don't force yourself to write when you're not interested. And trust your excitement: You may pick up a manuscript you haven't looked at for months, and find you're adding notes, writing in the margins. A sentence erupts. A voice starts to speak. Questions that have been in your head like dead weight get answered without your knowing it. (A writing friend may have said that a couple feels colorless in a particular passage. She suggests telling what they are wearing, or writing some dialogue. You try both of these suggestions and they don't fit the passage. Suddenly you're feeling the couple as they enter a room and simultaneously grab for a letter on the floor. Her arm arcs, his hand pounces—a violent, deliberate motion. It was this aliveness, not visual description that your friend was missing.)

On the other hand, you may stare at material for hours and think of nothing. Your efforts are wooden—a collage of false voices, meaningless sentences. Sometimes something happens in these uninspired moments, which is why it's occasionally worthwhile to try to revise even when you're not inspired. But if nothing happens, put the manuscript away and try not to feel discouraged. Revisions are like invocations for rain. You can do some rain dances, but you can't make the rain come.

The more attuned you are to your own rhythms for revising, the more likely it is that you'll be able to reenter the creative dream of your story. Just as there are right moments to approach a lover, their are right moments to approach a story—moments when you're feeling receptive, passionate, ready for adventure. Try to gauge for yourself when these moments are. Be sensitive to your body and your instincts. And *always* respond when inspiration strikes.

Gaining a sense of your creative rhythms is crucial to reenergizing your raw voice. What seems to work best for you?

Immediate, urgent reimmersion in a story? A longer pause? How soon after you receive feedback does it feel natural to return to your story? Is there a pattern? If not, experiment with different rhythms. Be prepared to be surprised, but look for an underlying, organic sense of what's right for you.

Sometimes friends, editors, or teachers expect performances that work against your rhythms. If you're a seasoned writer, you'll probably find ways to pull through in a pinch. And even if you're not, you can enjoy the challenge. But try, as much as possible, to respect your needs and get the world to respect them too.

How to Surprise Yourself in the Middle of Your Story

No surprise for the writer, no surprise for the reader.

— R O B E R T   F R O S T

Most exciting writing happens as a result of working with the unknown. The discoveries you make while you write energize the characters, the images, and the action. This is communicated as energy and momentum to the reader: A character you pegged as evil turns out to be compassionate. An adventure into the unknown results in a confrontation with something familiar. There's a hidden story that erupts in the middle of the apparent story, and the two stories reverberate. In a sense, the failure of the intended story is often the success of the realized story.

When this surprise occurs, you can usually feel it: There's an explosion of language in your head, a sense of space in the story itself curving like a Möbius strip, a sense of releasing tension. In a first draft, however, writers often stick too close to the story they wanted to write. They haven't surprised themselves. They've failed to discover something. The reader senses this as a lack of energy, motion, or transformation. "Nothing seemed to happen" is a common response.

To make something happen, you have to deviate from the intended story and write at the edges of the known. This is often a risky proposition, and indeed, it's probably one of the reasons writers are willing to spend hours writing lifeless, utterly safe revisions. What if you start writing a story you never wanted to write, and end up with characters you never wanted to meet? What if you find out something you don't want to know? What if you take a wrong path, and waste your time?

Ultimately, you have to take these risks. You have to steer yourself down an unknown path and leave your map behind. You can't force yourself to make discoveries, or be surprised. You can, however, set up conditions which set you on the path to the unknown and encourage you to improvise. Here are a few ideas that may get your story moving.

1. Inject a new element in the story—an argument, a sense of romance, a different landscape or texture, a sudden visitor. Also (with caution), consider some of the things we suggested in Chapter Thirty-two on plotting, and try injecting something quite dramatic—death, murder, a hurricane. See what happens. A story I wrote about soldiers painting a fake landing strip in the desert during a war was steeped in the textures of sand and heat. It felt tactile, but one-dimensional. Then I read a newspaper story about a perfume factory that had been bombed. When I injected this detail into the story, the shattered bottles and the scent of perfume added a rich counter-texture to the desert dryness.

2. Change the structure of the story. Think of the outcome that you planned, and reverse it. Start the story with the climax. If you've used flashbacks, omit them. If you've written scenes chronologically, mix them up. If the scenes move with fluidity (but perhaps predictably) forward, chop them up. Leave out the scene you think you most need.

3. Let your voice take the lead: work only with what interests you and has urgency. If a story is dull, but one or two scenes are exciting, even if they seem irrelevant to the story you wanted to write, it's a good bet that the first draft was a way of getting to these scenes and the rest of the story was a lot of throat-clearing. Use only these scenes as a basis for the rewrite. (Hint: Don't feel you have to produce pages of writing to earn a scene that excites you. Try starting with it!)

4. The same principle holds for phrases, sentences, and images that leap out with sudden numinosity. Consider throwing everything else away and using only this material as the building blocks for your next draft. (Note: We've emphasized these points many times, but they are invaluable tools for revision.)

5. Earlier, we suggested reading your story over, listening for shifts in voice, mood, and narrative. When you're revising, if you notice a shift, be sure to spend some time with it, even if it's jarring. It may conceal a hidden story, or a new direction. For example, I once wrote a story about a man who carries a folding chair with him wherever he goes. The story, told from the point of view of a woman bartender in a New England town, starts one evening when the man arrives at the bar with his chair. The opening moved along briskly, until the woman began to engage in a lengthy flashback about her life and the voice shifted. As I sat with this shift, I realized I was controlling the couple, preventing them from interacting. Suddenly I felt the man move forward and heard him ask: "Would you be willing to serve the chair a drink?" The woman answered, without skipping a beat: "Of course. Does it like the same dry white wine that you do?"

6. Change the person, tense, or point of view. As we said in Chapter Twenty-six, the point of view you start a story with is almost invariably the right one and the story somehow sounds wrong when you shift. This works the same way with tense, too. Nonetheless, sometimes you see new angles on a story when you experiment with writing a few scenes in a different person (first person instead of third), tense (present tense instead of past), or point of view (from the doctor's viewpoint instead of Mabel's).

7. Discover images that are evoked for you as a result of the story. Scan your memory for people the characters remind you of, places, objects, and events that recall your past. If you find something interesting and significant, see if this allows you to go deeper into your story (for example, enrich your descriptions, create more aspects to a character).

8. Try writing the whole story or complete chapters in one sitting, using less time than you think you need. A sense of urgency and compressed time can encourage loss of control, and you may end up surprising yourself.

Filtering Feedback

It's Monday evening at about eleven-fifteen and you're staring at the TV watching a mindless program with your legs stretched out in front of you. Now you're sitting in a comfortable chair, but you have a dreadful backache from sitting on a hard floor and lumpy pillows earlier in the evening. And your most recent story is in the garbage pail.

What's been happening?

You've just come back from a writing group.

There's an art to working with feedback. It takes a special kind of alchemy to absorb other people's opinions in a useful way—particularly when you're getting a lot of contradictory messages or vehement opinions that don't resonate. It's easy, even energizing, to dispense advise. But ultimately, you, the writer, must transport the feedback back to the alchemical boiler room and come up with concrete solutions—or reject the feedback as irrelevant.

It's useful to remember that the person you try to become when listening to feedback isn't the same person who's going to revise your story. You may nod your head at suggestions that seem utterly off the wall ("Make Millicent cross-dress!" or "Turn that four-page story into a novel!"). And when people are through, you smile and say, "My that was helpful!" Fortunately, this reasonable, socialized being isn't the person who's going to decide what to do with the feedback. *It's the writer who will decide, and the raw, reenergized voice of the writer who will write.*

Merleau-Ponty has said: "The writer is like the weaver, working the wrong side of the cloth." But this is a relative statement. People who read your story are also working on the wrong side of the cloth. They don't know what it feels like to have written your story from your side of the loom. For this reason almost everything that anyone tells you about your work is always slightly distorted. You must compensate for this distortion, the way you do when you look through a piece of wavy glass. You do this by reentering the trance, the dream state, of the story. Then you can feel, from the inside, the sense or nonsense of what's been suggested.

You also need to understand some basics about the art of feedback, and alert yourself to common mistakes people make when dispensing advice. Navigating through a labyrinth of suggestions is like navigating a foreign city: Your instincts are highly important, but so is a good map, with translations.

1. First, remember that when getting feedback, you need feedback from the story editor first. This is the editor with trenchant insights about the total energetics of your story, about dramatic tension, momentum, and transformation. Your story can't survive without these elements. They're the heart and lungs of your fiction, and should always be examined first. Beware of anyone who hasn't cultivated this editor and who begins by giving you feedback from the detail editor or the sentence editor. This is like a doctor inquiring how often you file your nails when your blood pressure is 230/180. Ask readers to look at the whole organism first, at the whole sweep of the story. Test the vital organs: character development, conflict, tension. Look at the overall color and tone. Don't stay in a feedback group in which people consistently give you feedback from the detail or sentence editor while ignoring the important wisdom of the story editor.

2. Everyone has his or her own fictional preferences. Always put feedback through this filter, and be careful of readers who impose their idea of what a story should be on your work. Every story generates its own standards of criticism. A Gothic romance or suspense/thriller can't be judged by the standards of a literary novel. A multigenerational epic can't be judged by the standards of a minimalist short story. Make sure your reader understands what each particular story is doing, and takes it on its own terms.

3. Along the same lines, be wary of suggestions about what to put into your story. Other people love to write your stories for you—it's easier than writing their own. Often even the most well-meaning person is unwittingly telling you to write the story *they* would write. Listen with a jaded ear. Try to get readers to talk in terms of what's on the page—what works and doesn't work for them. Ask them to identify weak spots, or places where there's potential for development, or passages where they felt something was missing. Remember that it's often easier for readers to fill in the gaps with their own story then to identify these spots. Yet your revision is generally most successful if new ideas come spontaneously, in improvisation, from your raw voice. Let readers point a possible path, but go on the journey alone.

4. Remember, too, that most writers approach a story in terms of what catalyzes their own work. A plot-driven writer thinks about plot, a character-driven writer about characters. You may get perfectly good suggestions that don't seem useful because you approach writing differently. Don't be discouraged or think you don't know how to tackle a story.

5. Be wary, too, of people who psychologize about your process. (For example, people who say: "I think you stopped the story because you were scared. I *know* there's more.") Such suggestions are well-meaning, but often are intrusive and can make you feel more vulnerable and off-balance. They can also undermine your voice. Unless you really know them and trust them, get people to stick to the text.

6. Be skeptical when readers say they don't understand *why* something happened, or when they demand neat, logical explanations for a character's motives. Do you really know *why* you left New York and came to California in 1987? Or *why* you chose to get your fortune told at a street fair? Or *why* you decided to leave a ghetto street gang and spend your time at a chess club? We rarely understand the why of human affairs. We can speculate and gossip and create theories; but all we really know is that we've had a completely direct, if fleeting, experience of a mysterious human choice. We don't have to understand our lives in order to believe them. But we do have to *experience* them. The same is true of fiction. For this reason, when a reader asks *why* ("Why did Raoul leave George alone on the riverboat?" "Why did Jeanne paint her boots pink?"), it's an indication that *for whatever reason* the reader didn't have a direct and believable experience of a person, event, or relationship. That can be useful. If you think they're right, reimmerse yourself in the material and create a more direct experience. (This usually happens as a result of you, the writer, experiencing the material more deeply and honestly. It almost never comes about as a result of adding explanations about your story or your characters.) Make sure you've used concrete details, sensate images, particular times, and places. Be honest about your characters. Develop relevant ambiguities. And above all, when someone says they don't understand *why*, don't rush back to your manuscript with editorial comments, expository dialogue, or flashbacks. They'll rarely come from raw voice and writing these things dutifully may cut off your access to inspiration.

7. Try to translate unhelpful criticisms into direct questions that you, the writer, can use. If your reader says she doesn't understand why so-and-so did such-and-such, ask if she felt, when the story was over, that *something* had happened. If so, what? This may provide important clues about what comes across to your reader and what doesn't. If your reader feels a scene is unnecessary, ask what might be lost if you took it out. If your reader hates a particular character, ask if there's a side to this character she enjoys.

8. It's always useful to find out the difference between what you intended to put across and what your reader heard. Sometimes the discrepancy is exciting—you discover you'd done more than you thought you had with your story. Then again, you may discover that your story is only half-written. Much of it remains in your head—vivid for you, but only partially visible to the reader. This gives you valuable insight about where to go back and flesh out a scene or character or relationship.

9. You know instinctively what helpful feedback feels like: It takes your story on its own terms, making suggestions to deepen or enliven what you already have. The reader is remarkably able to empathically enter your imaginative vision and encourage the story's fullest potential. You know how different this feels from feedback that strikes a discordant note, feedback that feels outside of your intentions, your sense of people, or language. Yet sometimes, over time, what sounded at first like dissonance, becomes fresh and exciting, and opens a new direction. Always be prepared to be fooled by your initial responses.

10. Genet said: *Find out what people most despise in your work and then push it to the hilt.* Always consider this possibility when dealing with feedback.

11. If you can't figure out how to incorporate the feedback into your story, don't worry. Think about it. Mull it over. Dream about it. If the feedback contains anything important, you'll incorporate it into the next story. Or in the story after that. The important thing is to keep on writing.

When to Rewrite from Scratch

The process of revision is one of intuitive judgment calls, and the more you revise, the easier these calls are to make. The easiest revisions by far are those that require only cuts. If your ear is good (in other words, if your sentence and story editor are well-trained), you can discover for yourself what to take out of a story: an explanation you don't need, a passage of flat dialogue, those sentences that are lovely but unnecessary. A good cut is instantly gratifying. You may have lost some of your favorite writing, but in exchange for some beautiful sentences, you'll possess a satisfying story.

Other stories require rewriting—or a combination of cutting and rewriting—all within the rubric of existing material. This usually requires a certain amount of tinkering. You may work best by going back into your story with a focused freewrite (a freewrite in which you launch yourself with trigger words or images). Or you may find that focusing on key characters or events and pushing them further (freewriting under pressure) is helpful. Or—without any prompting at all—a passage or scene may occur to you effortlessly in the middle of the night. These revisions are harder, but there's a sense of enormous relief and exhilaration when they fall into place. All those hours of frustration feel worth it.

There's another kind of story, however, that every writer is plagued with at one time or another—a story that no amount of scene-building, cutting, freewriting, or improvising seems to help. The more you work on it, the more unmanageable it feels. It's become a patchwork of different drafts, and though some passages sing, the whole is cut of too many different cloths. Reading it, you can feel the seams between the passages. You've gotten too much feedback, tried too many new ideas, rewritten scenes until they're dead. You've reached that critical point in revision where you've revised and tinkered so much, that you've lost the spontaneous energy of your voice. You're so far from your original, excited voice, that you simply can't recapture it. And the harder you try, the further away you get.

At this point it makes sense to wonder whether you should forget the story completely—or rewrite it from scratch. This is often a difficult decision, one that most writers decide intuitively. But the following questions can be helpful: 1) How committed am I to finishing the story *now* (as opposed to later)? 2) How committed am I to finishing the story *at all?* If you feel an urgency about finishing the story right away, this usually indicates that it's a good idea to stick with it. Some stories only get written because they *absolutely must get written at that very moment.* Other stories require time and a new perspective.

If you're committed to finishing a story right away and other methods of revision haven't worked, rewriting from scratch can be a liberating option. Put away those labored drafts. Take a short break, wait until you feel excitement, and then write the story as though you'd never written it before. (One writer I know swears that the best way to revise is to lose your computer disk— so you *have* to start fresh.) You forget those carefully crafted paragraphs you struggled so hard on, and let your voice simply tell the story. You're returning to raw voice, to inspiration, to your breath. You may stumble on new scenes, discard those you thought were essential. You'll often give the story a new beginning. And if the original story is still urgent, it will find its way back in the story you're writing. Sometimes a new story will emerge.

The second question—How committed am I to finishing the story *at all?*—is also important to ask, although you have to be careful not to answer it from the depths of discouragement. Every now and then a story can't be revised because your heart wasn't in it in the first place. The story may have felt clever or right for a certain market, or it may have echoed the voice of a writer you admire. But somehow the idea about the story never ignited with your voice, and there is no path—visible or invisible—from your inspiration to the writing. Almost every writer has made this mistake at one time or another, and it's important to be compassionate with yourself when this happens. It may turn out that doing something slightly unnatural will help you learn something about the craft of writing. Or you may have needed to exorcise a false and unhelpful persona. In any case, honest confrontation can only lead you more deeply to discovering the writer you really are.

In general, the path from inspiration to voice can be elusive, and occasionally leads you astray. (This is why rewriting from scratch is sometimes the only recourse.) It can also happen that significant events you've selected for a story—even though they reverberate and have valence—won't be the *right* significant events (that is, no matter how hard you work with them, they won't unpack or yield a narrative for this particular story). Sometimes a character can't live and breathe within the confines of a given conflict or situation. Or an image or phrase that has inspired you veers off in the wrong direction. The elements that help you get a story going are never guaranteed. Most of them truly ignite your voice. A few are false springboards. You'll never be sure until you try.

In the long run most impasses turn out to be navigable: strange detours on the path to a better story. Some impasses feel terrifying—like the moment before being pushed off a cliff. Others feel black and oppressive—like being locked in the trunk of a car. It helps to remember that all writers experience these impasses. Sometimes it's useful to describe them—and even impute them to characters. Most impasses have a small space inside of them that allows you room for motion. If you arrive at one, don't be frightened. Know that you'll be able to find your way beyond it. And know that it's okay to take your time.

Talking to the Stranger: Another Angle on Revision

When you start to work on a story, it's a private matter. Ultimately, though, a story becomes a communication, a letter of sorts, to a reader. Sometimes you get stuck on a story because you can't make a connection to your reader. You don't know whom you're writing to or what your intention is. Or you may be writing to an editor, a teacher, even a parent—an authority figure with the aura of an inner critic. So the question: Who am I writing to? is always helpful to consider.

I used to spend a great deal of time writing stories *for* my readers, or *at* my readers, but not *to* them directly. Can you comprehend the difference? My stories weren't letters or urgent messages. My readers were anonymous, just like I was trying to be. One day I asked myself how I thought of my readers: Were they fellow dreamers? Readers of a tabloid? People I was guiding on a journey?

My answer surprised me. "Guests," I thought. "I think of my readers as guests. And I think of myself as a host." This answer struck me as odd, because I'm not that comfortable giving parties, and I'm a conventional, nervous host.

The more I thought about this, the more I realized that the parties I wanted to give for readers were different from the parties I gave in real life. In real life, my parties were "nice," without any surprises. There was candlelight, dulcimer music, good food, soft, witty conversation. In my stories, someone might blurt out a secret just when dessert was served, a woman might appear at the door wearing antlers, two guests would flee the buffet to make love in the linen closet. These were parties that disrupted people, parties I felt apologetic about giving.

"Why don't you start your stories just the way you start your real parties?" I thought. "Light candles, play dulcimer music, do everything you can do to put the nervous host at ease. But don't pretend that the party won't turn into something strange or bizarre. Make the atmosphere as inviting as you want. But know where you are going."

This was a good suggestion. It allowed me to use the very marrow of my fear to ease into my story. It allowed me to access my voice, a voice talking *to* someone, a voice with an intimate purpose. This voice connected me to my reader and led me into my story.

As I felt safer, I got braver. Sometimes my parties started on a less comfortable note right away. Guests fled the table immediately. Men glowed in the dark by the second page. Yet now, surer of my intentions, I kept going, feeling a connection to the reader. These days, whenever I have trouble revising a story, I always ask myself: What kind of party do you want to give? It's not a magic question. Sometimes it doesn't help me find my story. But more often it does. I find a voice that connects to a reader, a stranger who is also a quest.

For you, meeting your readers may not have anything to do with parties, or hosts, or guests. It may involve making love on a train, dreaming a common dream, telling secrets in the dark, meeting at a fairground in a foreign country. Ask yourself what kind of connection you want to make to your reader. Even if you don't want to make any connection at all, it will tell you something.

A friend once told me he also felt quite apologetic about his stories: "Ultimately," he said, "I want my readers to feel like they're in a cold stubble field, listening to the wind, cold to their bones. They are very frightened and uncomfortable and at the same time they're so fascinated they can't get up until the story is over. In real life, I'm so *nice*. When I write I become a mean person, a spiteful trip-leader."

"So *be* nice," I said. "Create an apologetic narrator. Start your stories tentatively. Use whatever you are feeling to start your story. That will get your readers to come to the stubble field."

You may never meet your readers or know the conclusions they draw about your work. But they may become invisible allies as a result of the way you imagine them following you into your stories. Every time you write a story, you show a facet of yourself to your readers, and your voice is the vehicle for this facet. In fiction, voice never speaks in a vacuum. It speaks to another person.

Keeping Voice Alive

CHAPTER FORTY-SIX

Returning to Raw Voice

Every morning when Josshu
Woke up, he asked himself: Master! Are
you home? Then he would reply:
Master! I am home!

— A ZEN KOAN

The more I write, the more I tend to lose myself in my stories and forget about voice altogether. But I find it helpful, again and again, to return to working with my voice, as though it's a musical instrument that needs occasional tuning. It's helpful to do this during dry periods, for warm-ups, and for sudden periods of silence. Here's an example of a way I sometimes work:

This morning, a Tuesday morning in mid-June, I don't feel like writing at all—although I wouldn't say I was in a dry spell. Yesterday I got news that one of my friends is very ill, and this morning when I woke up I felt a tightness in my stomach and heard the words "desolation wilderness." "Don't think too hard about that," I told myself. "You have a lot of work." But now I'm sitting at my desk, looking at the wild, tangled garden outside my window and language feels like an assault.

For a while, I look at my garden—its lush uncultivated pear tree, its sun-dappled ivy, its riot of nasturtiums. I'm thinking about my friend (in spite of myself), and following the ache in my heart. Suddenly I'm writing:

When I was a kid, living in the concrete prairie of sub-urban Illinois, I found a secret garden. There weren't any gardens near our apartment building—just a vacant lot in back, filled with stubble and trash; but one day I noticed a small raspberry bush there—the smallest I'd ever seen, with a single wild raspberry growing on a branch. I raced to my bestfriend's house, showed her the bush, and made her the only other member of The Secret Garden Club. For a couple of weeks we came to the lot every day and sat quietly around the raspberry bush, looking at the raspberry. "Should we eat it?" Dee Dee asked. "No, never," I answered. Dee Dee had never read **The Secret Garden** *and was much less impressed by the raspberry than my desire to turn life into fiction. When the raspberry withered, the club disbanded.*

For a moment, I was right back in the flat landscape of Illinois, walking through a vacant lot filled with stubble. Before the rush of words *single wild raspberry,* there was an instant where I was just looking, with no words at all. When I surfaced, language felt friendly again. By following my mood, I'd transformed it. And by allowing my thoughts to wander, I found a missing piece of myself—something I needed in order to get going.

It's easy to forget that voice isn't a disembodied sound mechanism—that it's attached to a living, breathing person with preferences, passions, and moods, all of which influence writing. This is easy to forget when you start writing seriously. It's just as easy to forget after you've written for a while and think you've gotten beyond what you have experienced as "raw voice." Here are some things that help you remember that you're the source of your voice and help you keep voice alive:

1. From time to time return to keeping journal entries in which you write down memories of your day. Allow them to be trivial.

2. If your writing has evolved into stories that occur mostly in the third person, take time to write simple journal entries and anecdotes in the first person. Do the same if you usually write in the first person.

3. Experiment with not rushing to explain or wrap words around your experiences. Pause one second longer before making a decision about a person you meet for the first time. Don't try to understand an image in a dream. Tolerate silence before language.

4. Take time to listen to bodily sensations, and follow the images they suggest, even if you think "that's something I used to do, and it's not useful anymore. . . . "

5. Every now and then, ask yourself: "Who's writing?"

Voice over the Long Haul

Voice is never static. As you change, your voice will change. I saw this vividly when, not too long ago, my study reached a point of near anarchy. I spent a weekend cross-legged on the wooden floor, thumbing through old files, trying to reorganize. I pulled out sheaves of paper, marked with rusted paper clips or torn from a spiral notebook. Scribbles from an interrupted dream in the middle of the night. Lines dashed off in slanting blue pen, drafts from my old typewriter with the uneven type on erasable paper. Then my first computer, with its dot-matrix printer like some faded code. In moments I was deep in the archives, scanning manuscripts I hadn't looked at in years.

I quickly forgot about which shelf would hold what manuscripts, or whether I should use an alphabetical or calendar system for my files. Which was probably just as well. I was hearing voices from the past—my own. All those lyric, heartfelt poems and stories of my twenties, some that made me groan, others with lines that leapt out at me: "Wow, I wrote that?" And the stronger, surer ones of my thirties. I could see the greater authority, the shift that comes from sheer practice.

I felt connected to this person from the past. I knew her intimately. Yet she was distant from me. I remembered then something a friend of mine, an older woman, once said. "I still love those early stories I wrote, but I wouldn't want to still be writing them."

I couldn't still be writing them. I'm not the same person. At twenty I was so busy discovering who I was, I couldn't see beyond my inner landscape. I wrote all these abstract, soul-searching meditations. My voice reveled in metaphoric images of blackbirds and wheat fields (I'd never seen a wheat field!)— impassioned moments of reflection. Now I'm less patient with lyricism and more interested in people's stories, in the jostling of the everyday world. But the earlier voice led me to the later one.

One piece evoked a particular memory. I had dashed off some lines one day, typed them up to look like a poem, and shown them to a friend. "Is this a poem?" I asked. I had no idea what a poem was. Was anything you wrote in those jagged left-justified lines a poem?

He laughed and said, "Sure." He didn't know anymore than I, but somehow I trusted him. (His simple answer was the beginning for me of trusting raw voice.) Rereading that poem, I remembered what it felt like to not yet have an understanding of craft. And I felt the connection I still have with that inexperienced writer. We're both trying to access raw voice, to trust what comes up spontaneously, and to be open to an inner honesty.

With time, there's the confidence that comes from laboring in that room alone, day after day, learning what language can do (though there are still times I want to ask my friends if I've written a story or not). And there are other changes. A greater impatience with what's decorative, a greater urgency about what really matters. You shed mannerisms, become more relaxed. You drive harder to the heart of things. Your voice becomes more confident, more careless.

There's a flip side to this new ease and confidence. After

you've written for a while you may have to fight habit more vigorously. You've learned how to shape a story, how to create character, and it's tempting to slide into automatic. You know you can do something well. It's easy to just keep doing it.

At these times, you have to challenge yourself to avoid self-imitation. You have to be open to change, to be willing to return to that earlier time of confusion, when you didn't know what you were doing, or what a story was. When I write something that falls into place, that congeals, I know I've earned it. When I write something that mystifies me, I know it's something to pay attention to.

To keep voice alive and new, you not only have to continue to access raw material, you have to continue to take risks. These may be different risks. Risk taking after you've written for fifteen years may have less to do with dangerous self-revelation (or with writing at all!) and more to do with new subject matter, the need for a new vision. Jane Austen, in her later work (and after being disappointed in love), let a much darker view of marriage pervade her writing *(Mansfield Park, Emma),* than she had conveyed in her earlier novels *(Sense and Sensibility, Pride and Prejudice)* which were gay, spirited celebrations of young love. Interestingly, in her earlier work there was always a minor character with a "bah humbug" attitude toward romance—usually an older bachelor. It's as if this minor character is finally allowed to move center stage, and become the main voice of the novel (Fanny Price or Emma Woodhouse), giving full expression to attitudes that were only niggling, minor sentiments when Austen was younger.

L I S T E N I N G   F O R   V O I C E   S H I F T S

Significant shifts in voice are often preceded by a time of silence. (Twelve years elapsed between Austen's early novels and her later ones.) You may feel blocked, or just not feel like writing, or feel that you need to be quiet for a period of time. Maybe everything you write feels predictable, and you know you need fallow time. These unanchored periods can be scary, but if you're receptive and trusting of these changes, you may find yourself hearing a difference in the way you use language, or stumbling on some wholly new interesting accidents.

Sometimes a new persona is trying to emerge, as an earlier version of yourself is played out. Anne Rice talks of this when she says she no longer feels the need to write as Anne Roquelaure. She's written novels under three different names: Anne Rice for her Vampire chronicles, Anne Rampling for her contemporary fiction, and Anne Roquelaure for her pornographic writing. Her recent works, *Queen of the Damned* and *The Witching Hour,* she says, have drawn on all three voices. She feels her various personae have blended together.

This kind of evolution is as natural as shedding skin. Your voice will evolve as you evolve. You have to constantly grow beyond yourself. Letting this changing person emerge through your voice is crucial to your work with voice over the long haul. To be receptive to your voice's natural shifts, try these strategies:

1. If you feel the need to retreat from active writing for a while (maybe you've just completed an intense cycle of work, or maybe you're simply losing steam on work that's underway), honor this impulse. Often a time of nonwriting is an essential creative period in which underground forces are at work. Silence can be a fruitful part of your evolution as a writer.

2. Whether you're actively writing or not, in these periods that have a vague transitional feel, keep a journal or jot down stray fragments of voice that surface. Observe with interest, nonjudgementally, the feelings you express in your journal or the fragments of voice. Don't feel that you have to understand what's going on with yourself personally or creatively.

3. If you feel a voice surfacing which is new, always pay attention, even if it feels off-the-wall or silly, or not like your voice. It may be signaling a new direction. Play with this voice.

Write letters to it, asking where it lives, what it thinks about the work you're currently doing. Have it write back to you.

4.   If you feel the hint of a new persona inside you, write a monologue in the voice of this persona. Or, if this new persona still feels vague, go back to doing freewriting exercises each day, and don't think about what might be surfacing. In time, you may begin to recognize a voice that writes differently, begins to tell you new stories.

Audacity and Ruthlessness: (De)Constructing a Writer's Life

To develop your voice over the long haul, you have to develop a life that supports your voice. Certain conditions will help your voice thrive; other conditions will curtail voice. You may need a stable home life and a partner who brings you hot mint tea at the end of each evening of writing, or the freedom to haunt bars and clubs at all hours of the night. You may need the solitude of a quiet room or the screech and clamor of subways and coffee shops. You may not need much—a room where you won't be interrupted, a desk with a lock, a writing friend who understands you—but without this nourishment, voice won't flourish.

Think for a moment about what helps you to write freely, powerfully. What are the most important conditions for you? Make a list of what you need: stability? Moments of reckless abandon? Family? The freedom to travel? Isolation? How much time? How much material security? What kind of emotional support? From whom? Only by knowing what you need and insisting that you get it can you make room for your voice.

Sometimes your life may seem to shape your voice. Raymond Carver wrote very short stories because, with a family to support, he didn't have time for anything longer. If you have to write with three kids banging in and out of the room, demanding peanut butter and honey sandwiches, you learn to do so. Somehow your stories come out anyway. One of the reasons I wrote poems during those crazy years when I was a single parent, working and going to school, was because they were short. I could actually finish something in the bits and snatches of time I had late at night to work. (Poems are also great to write in a semiconscious, dazed state.) Every writer has certain circumstances that he can't readily change, and if you convinced yourself you couldn't write until the kids went off to college and you had a secure income, you'd simply never write.

But there are things you can control or change, and knowing what these things are is important. Go back to that list you wrote of what you need in order to be able to write. Next to each item, write a list of the things that get in the way. Include both big things (I have to work full-time to support a family; I have a sick mother-in-law to care for) and little things (I don't have my own room, I have to fix my motorcycle). What things on this list can you overcome? What things can't you change? Are you sure?

Next to each item that gets in the way of your writing, put down what you would need to change the situation. For instance, you may have said that you need to write in the morning when you're fresh, but you have to leave for your job by 7:30 A.M. To change the situation: I'd need to go into work an hour later. (Impossible.) I'd need to get up an hour earlier. (Even more impossible.) Now say about this thing: *I deserve this. I insist on having it. No one is going to get in my way.* If you deeply believed what you just said, would it make a difference? Would you be able to get that thing your voice needs to thrive?

Sometimes writers have to be ruthless, audacious, to get what they need. You have to be demanding. You have to be willing to have friends and family misunderstand. Perhaps you have to be willing to see yourself in a new way. You're a writer. That comes first. This belief in the self isn't always easy. There are a lot of messages that convince us we should do other things before we write. It's easy to see writing as a luxury, not a necessity. Yet this commitment to the self as a writer is crucial to the development of your voice. If you don't make room for your voice, you'll hear only occasional underground mutterings—those promises of stories that will never get written.

Not too long ago a writer friend of mine told me he had cancer. He wasn't sure he'd be able to finish his novel. I was stunned, even disbelieving. He looked the same as always, tanned, a bit paunchy. He didn't carry that dry, air-blown look of someone ill. On some level, though, his words hit me like a shotgun.

An astounding change came over me. The next morning I was at my computer pounding out the first chapter of a novel that I'd been carrying in my mind for some time, but hadn't thought I could get to for years. I confess I lost steam after the fourth chapter. My friend had surgery, was out of danger, and suddenly I had to write letters or do client work in the morning. But now when I complain that I don't have time to work on a novel, I look at those four chapters, written in fear and urgency, and remind myself that if it was the most important thing for me to do, I could certainly do it.

It's really about priorities, isn't it? And the belief in self that lets you exercise those priorities. If it helps, write a letter to yourself, presenting an irrefutable case for why you must have a new computer and two hours in the morning to work (or whatever it is you need). Or exorcise your demons: write down all the reasons you shouldn't insist on what you need. Then get to work. You'll always have doubts. It's how you handle those doubts that makes the difference between the person who develops his voice and the person who doesn't.

Don't create unrealistic demands that you can't possibly meet, that become an excuse not to write. But don't let the world roll over you either. Take a stand as a writer. Tell your friends not to call you during your writing hours—and don't answer the phone if they do. Help your neighbor buy groceries after you've put in your writing time, not before. Say no to that speaking engagement, that extra business trip. And insist on those things you need: a new book, a walk through an unfamiliar part of your city, a trip to New Mexico to do research, the freedom to sit and do nothing for an entire morning. As you nourish yourself, you're feeding voice.

The Writer as Character

Writers are wonderfully adept at mythologizing themselves, at creating themselves as larger-than-life characters. The cold truth is that much of what we do is unromantic, hard work. We sit by ourselves in a dusty garage day after day, hair uncombed, self-doubts teeming. To cheer ourselves and save face with the world, we turn ourselves into characters. We cultivate a writing persona whose mysterious or flamboyant or romantic image salves our doubts and deflects that worst of all questions: "Why don't you do something worthwhile?"

How do you present your writing self to the world? As a frantic, overburdened housewife who dashes off brilliant prose while breastfeeding? An intense lyricist who haunts jazz clubs and sees through the superficialities of life? A witty urbanite with wild hair and a bemused view of life who is always the life of the party? Write a character sketch of your fictionalized self, exaggerating your hallmarks.

Your writing persona can be a powerful and protective camouflage that enables you to write. Mobilizing this persona, you're able to hurl yourself into a role with abandon. (Actors often practice a role using masks; stronger emotions are released behind the protective shield.) Sometimes you write precisely in order to reinvent yourself, to open the door to a different creature—to nocturnal habits, shocking thoughts.

But these personae can also lead to rigid, even superstitious ideas about who you are as a writer, as well as how you work. (I don't write silly things. I can only write at night. I can't work if I get interrupted.) Sometimes you have to shatter the demands of your fictionalized personality to give your voice the freedom it needs.

When you cast yourself as a particular character, it's hard to play outside that role. A powerful persona can erase inner ambiguities and contradictions—those rich, gray areas your voice needs to access as you write. The parts of you that are lonely, blocked, not polished, tired—these parts are often the most crucial to your voice. This is the self that takes on life as your carefully constructed persona fades. In fact, increased tolerance for writing in a state of tenuousness and insecurity is often what marks a more experienced writer.

There's a scary vulnerability to the self stripped of a public persona. And there's a lot of power. By claiming these ordinary, disheveled parts of yourself, you get to use them in the service of your story. You embrace things you've avoided, reach a fuller range for voice to draw on. You're breathing from your diaphragm, not just your throat.

ANOTHER ENTRANCE
TO VOICE

Working with yourself in your life—your writing persona, your writing habits—is as important to voice as working with yourself in your fiction. When you work with yourself in your story, you call up emotions, dredge memories, listen to bodily sensations, and project these into your story. But you, yourself, are sitting at your desk. You're doing inner work. When you work with yourself in your life, you project this inner work into the world. You work with the symbols and badges of your public self—all the props of your daily life. You throw away your Virginia Slims. You write on the subway.

For one day, become a fly on the wall in your own life. Watch your rituals, your habits. Write down all the things you do (or don't do) that bolster your writing persona. Then try spending a whole day breaking the mold. If you think of yourself as someone who can only write in the morning, when you're fresh, write in the middle of the night. If you think of yourself as someone who can never preplan a story, write an outline first. Begin to write before your usual morning ritual (coffee, newspaper, phone calls). Write carelessly if you're usually fastidious.

Challenging your habits—particularly those habits that bolster a certain persona—is a way to stretch and challenge your voice. For a long time I thought I couldn't write unless I was alone. My writing self was private. I needed the door closed and the phone machine on. I was secretly in awe of those writers who sat in cafés and knocked off their prose while tossing down *lattes* and trading witticisms with strangers. Clever, but not deep, I rationalized.

Fortunately for my writing, life impinged. More than once I had no choice but to finish a piece I was working on as my daughter and her friends tried to see who could throw the most toys out the second-story window, or with administrators calling to tell me the class I taught had been canceled at the last minute and it wasn't their problem if I couldn't pay the rent. I was startled one day when a friend commented on how lucky I was to be able to write in the midst of chaos. I guess I can, I thought. In fact, the kids' fights over purple-haired trolls that interrupted my writing were good for my voice. They relaxed it, brought it into the everyday world. I stopped equating writing with a furrowed brow and solitary walks along the foggy moors. I haven't abandoned my private office with the shades drawn. It's a needed refuge. But over time my persona as the serious, reclusive writer has eased, and so has my voice.

You have to get beyond a sense of preciousness about your life as a writer. Be willing to be playful, disruptive, self-challenging. By evoking, bending, playing with your writing persona, you'll encourage your voice to be yourself, rather than who you think you have to be, or should be. Here are some more challenges:

1. Write a quick, third-person sketch, featuring yourself as a character, describing an apocryphal writing day.

2. Imagine a distant relative, one you've heard horror stories about but never met, arrives on your doorstep one day and totally disrupts your writing life. Write the story that gets written in the midst of this disruption.

3. Write a story in a genre you've never explored—a western if you always write surreal short-shorts; a metaphysical drama if you write murder mysteries. Think of yourself as the kind of person who writes these stories as you write. Dress the part.

4. Imagine you're being interviewed about your writing. How will you dress? How do you want to be seen, as a person and as a writer? Adopt a persona that is the opposite of this, and write a sketch of the interview.

Writing during Hard Times

A voice with authority always has some scars, and you don't get scars without living through some hard times. Such times happen for all writers. In a single week you may get three rejection slips, have your most trusted friend tell you he doesn't like your latest story, and learn that another friend is HIV positive. You feel yourself freeze up, get distracted, or go dead inside. At these times voice can feel inaccessible. "I ought to be able to write," you think, and yet you don't.

It makes sense that you might not want to write during difficult times. Writing is an audacious act to begin with. It involves being intimate with a stranger, showing glimpses of your private face, your private vision—things that aren't easy even in the best of times. Yet during hard times most people want to withdraw. It can be hard to be fully present with people you know—maybe even with yourself. So how can it feel safe to risk intimacy with a stranger?

It's also the case that much of writing involves a curious sort of double-vision, in which writers live life and see it as potential material at the same time. But during a hard time, raw experience has a way of taking over. The ability to see the aspect of life that's resonant and metaphoric disappears. You're too close to yourself to gain that crucial perspective. Everything becomes a "So what?" story.

When you feel overwhelmed or defeated, or just plain "flat," unmotivated, remember that every writer feels this way at one time or another. Some writers battle these feelings constantly. You're not alone. But you *are* different. When I was going through a major breakup, I could hardly get myself to sit at my desk, and whenever I did, I could only get myself to write one thing—long, analytical reminiscenses about what I was losing. When a friend's marriage was breaking up, she wrote all the time; divorce, for her, was one long adrenaline rush. However, when this friend gets rejection slips, she's filled with self-doubts; somehow, in the face of rejection, I often feel fierce, and want to write another story.

No matter what it is that silences your voice, in these times of doubt and paralysis, the struggle is to rekindle the audacity that enables you to write. During hard times your inner critics may have a field day—they can leap on your moments of weakness like sharks. You're not only dealing with the rejection slip or divorce. You have to fend off your critical voices as well. This takes extra strength at a time when you're not feeling particularly strong.

What actually reenergizes your voice is often mysterious. But all writers who struggle through hard times are in their own way trying to develop an inner ally or coach who helps them rev up and believe in themselves: "You can do it. You have stories to tell. Your stories matter." This is a different kind of coach than the one who helped you when you were stuck inside a story. He doesn't give specific suggestions for working with a story, but helps in a more general way to get your spirits up, banish your critic, and make you feel like leafing through an old notebook, starting to work on a scene in a novel, sitting down at your computer.

I find that anything that cuts through isolation can be extremely helpful in reviving the inner coach. Once, when I was in the middle of a difficult work situation, and having severe money problems, I wrote a writer whom I trusted and asked if it ever happened that he just couldn't write. He wrote back that indeed, it did happen, more often than he admitted. Then he continued:

> *The malign paradox is that the fact that I cannot write always makes me even more unable to write, as I pull the loop closer and tighter than ever. Somehow, you see, it must be my fault; there must be something that, if I only did it right, would fix the problem, open the bottleneck. Since I can't seem to open it, I'm not doing it right, and therefore become more depressed. Which, of course, just exacerbates the problem.*
>
> — MICHAEL FARREN

When I read this, I felt relieved.

You may feel that allowing yourself to withdraw during rough times is what's best for you. Somehow you trust that your voice will be there again when the time is right. The longer you write, the better you'll know how to keep your voice alive, even in the face of huge setbacks and disasters. In the meantime, here are a few other things that can help you strengthen your inner coach, bolster your audacity, and reactivate your voice.

1. Spend fifteen minutes in the place where you usually write (your desk, your bed, your garden), without pressuring yourself to write. You can listen to music, draw, or conduct a small ritual (if it feels genuine to you), like placing some flowers or a favorite stone in this place. You can also just stare into space and daydream.

2. Read some journals of writers who have written honestly about their lives—including unproductive periods. (I've always enjoyed a single-sentence entry in one of Kafka's journals: "Today burnt some old disgusting papers.")

3. Read some biographies of writers that may give you a sense of the occupational hazards of the profession. The depressions of Virginia Woolf can be oddly comforting. And so can the triumphs over adversity. (I've always taken heart from the fact that when Lawrence Sterne's wife decided that she was the Queen of Bolivia, and he himself was a poor bankrupt preacher with TB, he locked himself in his study and wrote *Tristram Shandy,* what Johnson called "the longest shaggy dog story in the English language.")

4. Read writers who have used difficult events in their lives, or thorny aspects of their own character, for material. Marguerite Duras, who has published her journals of the Second World War, as well as the highly autobiographical book *The Lover,* is one good example. Raymond Carver, who used his own struggles with alcoholism for many of his stories, turns himself, at times, into a pathetic, unappealing character. He accepts that he didn't like himself. This acceptance reaches and relieves readers.

5. If you're feeling flat, allow yourself to observe your world. You don't have to record your observations. Just notice what you're seeing. You may discover that this flat, "So what?" feeling conceals an interesting perspective.

Take some time to remember that feelings of isolation during hard times are universal, and remind yourself that this is one of the reasons readers read and writers write. Even a close acquaintance may "turn off" when you're going through a hard time. Yet readers, safe in the comfort of their own rooms, really want to know what's going on, after all. This reader is the trusted stranger on the train, the person you want to talk to in the dark. Imagine this reader. If you want to, write your reader a letter.

Experiencing adversity can also help you to seek out people in your life who don't support the myth that life is a joyride. This doesn't mean gloomy people who don't know how to have fun, just honest people. And be open to the wisdom of strangers. About six years ago I had a serious accident in which my right elbow required two surgeries, and possibly a third—in part because I'd gotten careless medical treatment. I felt so handicapped, and was in such constant pain, that my voice closed up, and I interrupted a collection of short stories. One day at a party I began to compare surgical notes with an elderly man I didn't know very well. He told me about his hip operation and I told him about my elbow. "Just remember two things," he said. "First, that you'll get through it. And second, that no one else gives a good god damn. They really try. But they're just so happy it isn't them, they can't help it." There was surprising truth to this acerbic remark. It released me from a kind of lie I was living, a need to put on a "good face" about the whole experience. And I felt like writing again.

Some Truths about Truth-Telling

One fall day when I was about twelve, a plumber friend of my mother's appeared at our door hunched under a box of scrap wood. A swirl of leaves seemed to propel him into the room where he set the box on the hearth with considerable huffing. The scrap wood was a jumble of wooden toilet seats, painted white. "Shouldn't go to waste," he mumbled, and got to work building a fire. He bent on one knee, hooking those white seats into the flames, the paint spitting and flaring, and began to complain about his daughter's new boyfriend—a Mexican. "Not while she's living under my roof," he said. "No daughter of mine's going to go out with one of *them.*" I was appalled, and not by the toilet seats. My mother shushed me with her eyes. This is a friend of mine, doing us a favor. Don't challenge him. Be nice.

My mother knew the power of language. A simple sentence can destroy a friendship, disassemble a world. You can patch, explain, add footnotes, but sometimes you can't erase what's been spoken. Language has extraordinary, generative power. To speak something is to bring it into being—at least as a possibility.

Writers live with the same understanding of the power of truth. Sometimes this understanding empowers them. Sometimes it frightens and inhibits them.

Writers must invent extraordinary worlds and populate them with fascinating characters. But in order for these worlds to ring true, they must be saturated in something that *is* true. If they're not, the reader won't have anything to trust, and will refuse to suspend disbelief and enter your story.

For this reason, truth is the fiction writer's constant ally. It's what allows voice to imbue the imagination with life. The truth we're speaking of isn't the objective truth of mathematics, but the fierce surprising subjective truth of yourself, including your observations of other people. Sometimes you must confront deep indifference or painful memories. At other times you must break a taboo. Whatever these truths are, you must figure out how to work with them.

The capacity for truth-telling requires courage. It requires insisting on your right to confront things in yourself and in others as you see them—and then to write about them as you wish, in the privacy of your workroom. This kind of truth can lead you to forbidden territories—places where you've stashed your childhood cruelties, spitefulness, rages, and obsessions. Or it may reveal your more banal secrets—parts of yourself and your life you don't show to anyone. As a writer, you must be able to enter such forbidden territories; for as long as a landscape remains off-limits, it remains static. You can't explore it, and must avoid all paths that might lead you to it. But when you decide that you can touch the truth about anything, you shake a secret self awake: You find you can talk about things you never dreamed of, discover a story inside a story, tell an old story in new ways. Concealed ambiguities emerge. You see the landscape through all kinds of lenses. One truth leads to another. Your ability to invent increases.

Most writers acquire the courage to tell the truth in stages— and in this sense it's a blessing that there's usually such a long lag between writing and publication. The first time I wrote something true and forbidden, it was in illegible handwriting, and I hid it deep in a drawer. The next morning, I got up, laced my shoes, had coffee, and life went on as usual. Sometime later, I wrote about something else that seemed equally unspeakable. Again, nothing happened to me. Over time, with practice, I began to lose the sense that my creation could backfire, or become a Frankenstein monster.

That was the first stage. Later, I showed my work to other people, and even later decided what to publish. Over time, I began to ask myself questions about the difference between gossip, scandal, senseless self-exposure—and the sort of truth that cuts to the bone and illuminates. I still wrote everything I wanted to write. But I learned that I could set limits and didn't have to destroy others' lives or my own privacy to tell the truth.

There are times when you may choose not to publish material for the sake of someone else's feelings, and other times when you may choose to disguise a personal truth. There are other times when—in the service of art—you may risk hurting, angering, or alienating someone by publishing work that contains raw and possibly recognizable facts. These are personal, and often troubling, decisions for every writer. Nobody can decide them for you. But no matter what you publish, you must feel free to write whatever you want to in drafts that no one but you will ever see. This includes facts about yourself, stories you hear from other people, things that happened in your family. If you don't feel free to write about everything, writing becomes an overly cautious act. It's a bit like having a workroom with a closet full of extraordinary things and never being able to open the closet and look at them.

It's helpful to remember that people read fiction because they're hungry for truth. The pretensions of public life may be necessary—but by concealing so much of who we really are we perpetuate the myth that public faces and private faces are exactly the same. Secretly, everyone knows this isn't true. Yet at a party, or a high school reunion, or even a tense afternoon with a friend, it's easy to believe you're the only person with divorced parents, an unhappy relationship, unsatisfying work, sexual obsessions, or a messy apartment. Gossip is fun, in part, because it exposes this lie and provides relief—which is why tabloids are so popular. But writing that goes beyond mere anecdote and uses truth to dramatize the human condition can reduce loneliness, as well as entertain. This is the truth of wit and compassion. And readers are often grateful for this truth.

In *Annie John,* Jamaica Kincaid wrote about a daughter's relationship with her mother, and brought into bold relief what we all pretend we don't know: Parents and children don't get along the way sit-coms, commercials, and long chatty Christmas letters say they do. Neither the mother nor daughter emerged as evil. But they did reveal some basic bad feelings that most parents and children have experienced in their existence together.

We're not suggesting here that telling the truth involves a total transcendence of one's feeling about the experience. Writers are human beings, and this will imbue all work with human biases, including anger and even vindictiveness. Jamaica Kincaid didn't try to write a book that concealed her outrage. Nor did she bother to conceal parts of people's real identities. These rough, ragged edges make her story more believable. There's a real person for readers to identify with.

There are many kinds of truths for the writer to confront: the truth of family scandals. The truth of irrational convictions. The truth of fascination with deception. The truth of a vision of the future. The truth of a feeling that turns out to be quite ephemeral. The truth about a perception of a friend. Some of these levels of truth are surprisingly simple, although they take great courage to confront—as does the decision to break taboos. (*My brother came after me with a knife when I was seven. My uncle slept with my French teacher and made me promise not to tell.*) Some are more complex. They involve admitting points of view that have eluded you, heretical beliefs, demonic passions. Remember that facts and passions tend to work together. Writing with candor about certain facts arouses your passions; writing about your passions opens up areas of carefully guarded facts.

Above all, remember that learning to work with the truth requires time. Don't push yourself to write everything at once. Be honest and proceed slowly.

TRUTH-TELLING AND FAMILIES

It's not an accident that we began this chapter with a story about being unable to speak the truth in a family setting. Families are tight survival units, and usually have explicit and implicit rules about what can be told inside the family, what can be told outside the family, and what can't be told at all. Almost all of us emerge from our original families with a sense of knowing some unspeakable secrets and the belief that telling those secrets would constitute violating a taboo. And almost all writers, at one time or another, have thought of breaking such taboos. Not all taboos are there for the writer to break publicly. Some may need to be respected. But the writer's own workroom must be a place that is safe and protected—even from the gods—in the event that taboos are broken. Here are some questions and exercises that may help you sort out the taboos you learned about truthtelling:

I. Questions

1. Who was the storyteller in your family of origin? The myth maker? Were they the same person or different people?

2. What were the family myths? the family secrets? the family's favorite stories?

3. What were the rules about truth-telling? Who made the rules and how did you learn them?

4. Who was allowed to speak frankly? Who got to have a 'voice'?

5. How were people rewarded and punished for lying and/or telling the truth?

6. What lies were acceptable in your family?

7. Was there a particular setting or place where what was really going on was revealed or denied (dinner table conversations, holidays, family reunions, picnics)?

8. Was there any relationship between family secrets and family myths?

9. Was there a distinction between what sorts of things could be told inside the family and what could be told outside the family?

10. Ask yourself the same set of questions about truth-telling in your current relationships.

II. Exercises

1. Take one family myth and retell it, putting in what you think (or imagine) might have been left out.

2. Take a family secret and tell it first as a short descriptive paragraph, and then as a narrative with dialogue.

3. Become different people in your family; have each one tell his or her secrets.

4. Imagine the worst-case scenario should you violate a family taboo about truth-telling by writing about it, and then write about it. (Will your mother die? Your wife leave? Will God send down a lightening bolt and strike both you and your computer dead?)

5. Now imagine a best-case scenario, an ironic scenario, an absurd scenario, a melodramatic scenario, and a comic scenario. Write about them.

6. Tell part of a family secret truthfully. Lie, invent, and fictionalize the rest. Do the same thing with a family myth.

7. Become various people in your family. Have them write outrageous true confessions.

8. Not all taboos pertain to dramatic and scandalous events. There are also taboos about point of view and perspective (don't acknowledge anything funny or absurd—so what if

Uncle Marvin picked his nose non-stop at the unveiling of his mother's tombstone?). There are taboos about the powers of observation (don't look at the love bites on Grandma's arm). And there are taboos about subtle forms of disagreement (if your older sister offers you corned-beef hash three times after you've told her you're full, don't think she's a nag—she's a very generous person). Time-travel back to an ordinary family scene and look and listen carefully. Write whatever you experience. Again, go slowly.

The Importance of Lying

When I was a kid, I told lies to gullible baby-sitters. "My dad and mom are divorced. My real mom moved to Des Moines and won't tell me what she does. I think she might be an artist, but I'm not sure. I visited her once and she didn't let me see where she lived. She made me stay at a hotel. I think she was embarrassed." The baby-sitters may or may not have believed me, but they were fascinated.

The lies I told when I got into trouble were just as inventive. "Rosemary Newman pushed my books in the mud. She always does things like that. During recess she eats mayonnaise sandwiches. And she says she has a pet snake named Tounces. I think she's weird."

Lying is the flip-side of truth-telling. It's the "making it all up" part that gives a story juice. The writer Isaac Bashevis Singer told countless lies when he was a child in Poland. Once, on the first night of Chanukah, he went on a forbidden walk instead of coming home from cheder. He found himself in a strange neighborhood, went into a restaurant, and told a woman an outrageous lie about being an orphan—so outrageous she bought him a meal. "I couldn't keep from telling lies," he once said during a workshop I attended. "It was the beginning of becoming a writer."

Lying is often the leap that turns an anecdote into a story. If you embellish, allow yourself to spin a tale, real events become more than "just so" stories. They highlight some aspect of life and take on resonance. Yet writers often feel they can't change the facts because in real life "it didn't happen that way." Once I wrote a story modeled after my parents. A woman settles down for an evening alone, relishing take-out food and cheap magazines. When her suitor pays an unexpected call, she throws everything away before letting him in the door. After a dramatic beginning, the story bogged down. A friend suggested I insert some conflict to get the story going again. I said, "But that didn't happen." She said, "You often have to lie to tell a good story."

The material of your life is yours to claim and use. It's also yours to bend, stretch, mold, and change. Part of finding your voice is giving yourself permission to use your life and the lives around you for material—and then to distort that material outrageously. Events of your life can be a starting point. But you need to give your voice permission and range to draw on other events and lives as well as your own imagination.

In *Billy Bathgate* E. L. Doctorow based his material on something "real"; Billy Bathgate, a fictional character, gets involved with Dutch Schulz, who is a "real life" criminal, right up there with Al Capone. If out of some misguided need to confine himself to just the facts Doctorow hadn't allowed himself to create this fictional character, his novel would have been stillborn. And indeed this is exactly what happens when writers stick too close to the lap of their lives, or substitute research for writing and imagining. Basement shelves are filled with leaden products of such research, as well as faithful recounting of "real life stories," books that never get published because they weren't animated with a little lying.

There are thousands of ways to lie. In his stories, "The Other" and "Borges and I," Jorge Luis Borges speaks about meeting a man who is his double. And in her autobiography, *Family Sayings,* the Italian writer Natalia Ginsberg lies through an act of omission—by telling the reader very little about herself. We hear her mother, father, and brothers talking and arguing. We see how they look, where they ski, what they read. But we know almost nothing about Natalia Ginsberg and can only infer her grief when her first husband is killed by Fascists. It's conceivable that she was quiet as a child, and as the youngest in a large Italian family, experienced herself as being effaced, even without a voice in the family setting. But she must have fallen off her bicycle, disliked certain foods, and had private thoughts and opinions. Her absence, however, is an audible presence in the book—one of an invisible recording angel, with great powers of memory and observation. If she'd followed the dictum, "Whenever you write about your life, you have to tell us all about yourself," this book, which is now used in Italian schools to document the rise of Fascism, wouldn't have been nearly as effective.

To use the known as a springboard into the unknown, try this:

1. Narrate a short story from your life, but put a different spin on it: make it more tragic, more exciting, more pathetic. Add at least one event that never happened.

2. Imagine that your mother (or your father, or a good friend, or you) had a double life. Write a story in which you describe this other life.

3. Pretend you're a well-known fictional character, or a well-known politician or celebrity. Write about either your life or their life, but from their point of view.

4. Write letters to a double of yourself who lives in a parallel universe. Have the double write back to you.

5. Write a story about a lie you told when you were a child as if that lie were true.

6. Write about an event that you took part in and leave yourself out as a character. Pretend you were never there.

7. Write an acerbic letter to one of your elementary school teachers about the importance of lying.

Becoming Your Own Sovereign

Part of owning your own voice is having an irreverent attitude toward outside authority and a keen sense of your own. Your guess about how to write, how to live as a writer, how to get those stories to fill the page, is better than anybody else's. Maybe, when all is said and done, you don't believe voice is all that important. Maybe all you need to do is key into an exciting plot and launch yourself. Or maybe you have no theory at all about how you write and aren't interested in finding one. After I'd talked about voice for three hours in a workshop one Saturday, a man in the front row looked at me with an air of puzzlement and said, "I never think about voice at all. I just have this character, this man wearing an apron, and he starts talking."

A year and a half later, I was delighted when this same man phoned me for a consultation. He'd finished the story of Morris, that man wearing the apron, and wanted to send it to me. I spent an evening chuckling through his manuscript, which was impeccably typed and filled with italics and emphatic small caps. In his Bronx accent, Morris unraveled a story which began at a funeral, rolled through a stint as a volunteer literacy teacher, struck out for a shooting range, and slammed to a halt as Morris cracked a would-be robber over the head with a broom in a mall restaurant—never breaking stride. There was no question this writer had accessed an original, natural voice and told a remarkable story. I didn't ask him how he did it.

Only you can write your stories, only you can discover how to write them. Create your own improvisation for writing, for living. Deconstruct our book. Knight yourself as your own sovereign. Of your life. Your voice. Your stories. We're out here, waiting to read them.